MW00898697

Sales Funnel Management for Small Business Owners in 2019

Strategies on How to Setup a Highly Automated Funnel for Your Business (That Actually Makes Money)

Mark Warner

© Copyright 2019 - All rights reserved.

The content contained within this book may not be reproduced, duplicated or transmitted without direct written permission from the author or the publisher.

Under no circumstances will any blame or legal responsibility be held against the publisher, or author, for any damages, reparation, or monetary loss due to the information contained within this book. Either directly or indirectly.

Legal Notice:

This book is copyright protected. This book is only for personal use. You cannot amend, distribute, sell, use, quote or paraphrase any part, or the content within this book, without the consent of the author or publisher.

Disclaimer Notice:

Please note the information contained within this document is for educational and entertainment purposes only. All effort has been executed to present accurate, up to date, and reliable, complete information. No warranties of any kind are declared or implied. Readers acknowledge that the author is not engaging in the rendering of legal, financial, medical or professional advice. The content within this book has been derived from various sources. Please consult a licensed professional before attempting any techniques outlined in this book.

By reading this document, the reader agrees that under no circumstances is the author responsible for any losses, direct or indirect, which are incurred as a result of the use of the information contained within this document, including, but not limited to, — errors, omissions, or inaccuracies.

Dear Reader,

As an independent author,
    and one-man operation
    - my marketing budget is next to zero.

As such, the only way
    I can get my books in front of valued customers
    is with reviews.

Unfortunately, I'm competing against authors and
    giant publishing companies
    with multi-million-dollar marketing teams.

These behemoths can afford
    to give away hundreds of free books
    to boost their ranking and success.

Which as much as I'd love to –
    I simply can't afford to do.

That's why your honest review
    will not only be invaluable to me,
    but also to other readers on Amazon.

Yours sincerely,

Mark Warner

Table of Contents

Introduction

I want to thank you for choosing this book, *Sales Funnel Management for Small Business Owners in 2019: Strategies on How to Setup a Highly Automated Funnel for Your Business (That Actually Makes Money)*.

Common problems that a lot of small business owners face is a lack of time, a loosely targeted social media marketing strategy, and the lack of proper understanding of their target customers. These problems can affect your bottom line, and you might not even be aware of it. The good news is, these can be easily remedied by corrective action, and this is where this book comes in. The goal of this book is to help you solve these issues effectively and efficiently without burning a hole in your pocket. The actionable steps and tips given in this book are practical, easy to implement, scalable, and cost-effective. Do you wish to increase the efficiency of your marketing efforts but aren't sure where to begin? If yes, then this is the perfect book for you.

In this book, you will learn about different strategies you can use to create a highly functional and automated sales funnel, which will help the efficiency and the productivity of your business. The information given in this book is backed by research done by eminent personalities like Robert Cialdini, whose principles of persuasion are commonly used in marketing.

If you want to turn things around for your business, then it is time to take some action. Go through the information given in this book and implement the suggestions given so that you don't get left behind your competitors. In business, time is money, so it is essential to act quickly.

So, let us get started without further ado!

Chapter 1: Customer Buyer Persona

Unless you have never dealt with marketing before, it is quite unlikely that you aren't aware of the need to define your target audience. Having a detailed and thorough idea of your average customer improves the focus and target your marketing campaigns. You might think that a basic demographic profile of your existing customers will suffice, but that's not the case, and this is where the concept of buyer personas comes into the picture. A buyer persona is derived from your target customers. Instead of including just numbers and figures, a buyer persona takes into account the audience's research and is presented in the form of a hypothetical profile of an ideal customer. Think of it as a semi-fictional depiction of your ideal audience. For instance, instead of merely targeting your marketing efforts toward women in the age group of 25-35 years with an income between $45,000 and $80,000, you will be targeting Olivia, a 27-year old fashion designer.

Understanding your customers is quintessential for any business. A successful business owner not only understands what their customers want but also knows the most efficient means of making their products or services available to those customers. It means knowing more about their customers than their age, name, or income. As a business owner, you must know about your customer's interests, tastes, preferences, what they watch, where they spend their time, and the kind of content they read. All these things can be leveraged to increase the business's profits.

It is also essential to understand their buying behavior, too. As a business owner, you must try to understand the types of individuals who will need or want the products or services your business provides. Here are a couple of simple questions you must keep asking yourself daily to become a successful business owner.

- What is the reason for buying the products or services you offer?

- How frequently will they need to purchase that product or avail the service? If you take steps to be proactive in your marketing efforts around the time when the customers need to buy something, chances are they will not look elsewhere for the same.

- Is the buyer your ultimate consumer, or are they buying it for someone? The messaging and promotional strategies you design will depend on the ultimate consumer of the product or service.

- Where will they purchase the product from? Will they buy it from a brick and mortar store, or can it be ordered online, too?

Businesses that are aware of what their customers want and what their expectations are can use this information for customizing the buyer's experience to establish brand loyalty. A simple means to do this is by increasing the length of customer interaction your business usually has. By simply listening to what your customers want, and by answering the questions they typically have or solving any of their problems, you can create a better customer experience. To do this, you must be aware of what the customers are looking for. As a business owner, it is quintessential that you not only provide excellent quality services and products, but you must stand out from the other competitors in your niche. Your customer knowledge, along with relationships, gives you this advantage. So, developing a customer persona is the first step to create a successful marketing strategy. This, in turn, helps increase your profitability.

You might be thinking that you already have customer personas in place. Well, it is a common misconception that customer segments, and customer personas, are synonyms. Most businesses tend to create customer segments instead of personas. Segmentation enables a business to understand the various sets or groups of customers in the market. It might give you an idea of where a specific group resides, their age, or even their usual buying behavior. A customer persona enables you to understand these groups and recognize certain key traits present within which are favorable for your business.

To create an ideal representation of your sample audience, you need to create customer personas that are based on the analysis of your real customers. It helps create a detailed and thorough representation of your ideal customer which includes information like their personal motivations, the value they look for in a business, the kind of content they like, the communication they expect, etc. Businesses can use all these insights and incorporate them to create a customer experience, which is no longer one-dimensional.

Benefits of Creating Customer Personas

A characteristic of a good marketing campaign is that it focuses on your target audience. So, before you can develop a marketing strategy, it is essential to create a customer or a buyer persona. There are different benefits you can reap by creating customer personas, and they are as follows.

Right time and place

Having detailed customer personas while designing your marketing campaign is quintessential, especially because most businesses are client-oriented these days. It helps identify where your ideal customers spend most of their time. Instead of wasting your time on platforms seldom used by your target audience, wouldn't it be better if you target those platforms they do spend time on? Instead of blowing your budget on unwanted ads, you can create such content which will help solve a buyer's needs. Instead of spending money marketing on platforms where you think you can find your potential customers, you can now be sure of the platforms you must target. Being present at the right place at the right time is an invaluable resource for businesses these days.

Develop brilliant content

What business wouldn't want to develop brilliant content? The idea of marketing is to transform the "wants" of a potential customer and make them seem like "needs." Content is king when it comes to marketing. If the content isn't exceptional, it will become rather difficult to attract your target audience. To create such content, you must have a thorough understanding of your customer base. You must be aware of the questions they ask, the challenges they face, and the possible solutions they are seeking. By being aware of all these things, you can create content which will instantly appeal to your audience.

Prioritizing leads

Having established your customer personas, it gives a marketer a glance into the lives and minds of your potential customers. You can redirect your marketing efforts toward those customers and leads who are in sync with your business's customer personas. When you are aware of the customer personas and where they usually spend their time, you can target the digital ads in those areas instead of generating random ads.

Stand out from the crowd

By spending the necessary time on researching, building customer personas, and creating good content, your business can easily stand out from your competitors. A lot of businesses tend to spend a lot of time talking about their business, but only a few spend time answering the questions which their potential customers might be asking. When you shift your focus to your potential customers, you will be able to reach them before they even realize they need your business. By acknowledging specific problems your target customers might be facing and giving solutions to the same, your business essentially becomes a trustworthy source of information the customers come to rely on.

Once you create the customer personas, your job doesn't end there. You must keep updating the personas from time to time. We live in a dynamic world, and you cannot expect any different from your customers. When you keep updating the customer personas, it helps ensure that your marketing efforts are generating the returns you expect.

Customer Persona Examples

Now that you are aware of the different benefits you can reap by creating customer personas, let us look at a couple of examples, so you know what an ideal customer persona looks like. A customer persona doesn't have to be lengthy, as long as it includes all the necessary information.

Online shopping has become quite popular these days, and rightly so. Online shopping helps customers save time, energy, effort, and even offers attractive deals. Here is an example of a customer persona for an online business selling shoes.

Name: Rachel Smith

Gender: Female

Age: 35

Occupation: Receptionist

Earnings: Over $35,000

Location: Los Angeles, California

Motivation: Rachel tends to get rather emotional while shopping for shoes in regular retail stores since her feet are quite narrow, and she seldom finds any that fit her perfectly. Dejected with her offline shopping experience, she turns to online shopping. Online shopping allows her to filter her requirements and find an ideal pair. Apart from this, she can also compare the prices of shoes across different sites and read the reviews posted before making a purchase.

Goals: She needs a SS (4A) width shoe. Is keen to purchase multiple pairs for different occasions. Hopes to find shoes that provide both style and comfort without compromising on either.

Frustrations: Limited choice available when the width-filter is applied. No other recommended shoe option is shown to simplify the shopping process.

When the business is aware of what their target customer is looking for, it becomes relatively easier to deliver what the customer needs.

Here is an example of a customer persona a coffee shop can use.

Name: Sarah Geller

Gender: Female

Age: 20

Occupation: Student/ Freelancer

Earnings: $15,000

Location: Ohio

Motivation: Sarah is a student at the local university, and she likes to freelance as a content writer. She is looking for a place where she can work as well as study. Aims to find the ideal work and study environment which offers comfort along with good coffee and food.

Goals: She needs a place that serves good coffee at a reasonable price. A place that offers free Wi-Fi and offers good deals or coupons. It offers cozy and comfortable seating with plenty of charging stations and isn't noisy.

Frustrations: Inability to find all her requirements in one place.

Questions to Ask

Questions about the customer's background

Briefly describe the customer's personal demographics.

The best place to start developing your customer profile is by obtaining demographic information. It is not only easy to get but is the starting point of painting a more precise and accurate picture of your ideal customer. What is their marital status? What is their age group? What is their average income, and where do they reside? What is their gender? Do they have any children?

Write about their educational background.

What is their level of education? Which schools, colleges, or universities did they attend? Try to include specific names of the educational institutions.

Write about their career path.

How did they end up in their current job? Is the subject they majored in at school similar to their job profile, or is it different? Is their career path conventional or did they shift from one industry to another?

Questions about their work

What is their job profile or title?

How long has the customer held onto their current title or role? Does their job description include managing other employees, or are they an individual contributor?

Whom do they report to and who reports to them?

The seniority level of the customer in relation to developing the customer persona will depend on the product or service you are offering. If you are a B2C business, then this piece of information will help you gain insight into your customer's daily life. However, if you are a B2B organization, then this information comes in handy. Is your customer persona present at a director or a managerial position? The higher up in the organizational hierarchy your persona is, the more autonomy they have while making any purchase decisions.

How to measure their job?

What are the different metrics that your persona deals with? Which charts, numbers, or graphs does your ideal customer persona look at day after day? This information will help you understand what makes them successful and the things they might be anxious about when it comes to obtaining specific numbers at work.

What does a typical day in their life look like?

What time do they leave their homes to go to work, and what time does their workday end? What are their most productive hours during the day? What does a typical day at work look like? This information must include details about the way they spend their day at and outside their place of work. Do they spend more time at work or at home? Do they like their work? Is there any other place they would rather be? What are their hobbies, or what do they do in their spare time? What kind of vehicle do they own? Are there any specific TV series they like to watch? What kinds of clothes they usually wear? You get the gist, don't you? You can ask them personal questions as long as it pertains to their daily life.

What skills do they need to do their job?

If they had to hire someone as their replacement, then what are the skills required? What are the skills they possess to do their job? What are the ideal skills required to do the job and how well does your persona measure up? Where did they acquire these skills from? Did they get on-the-job training, have any previous experience, or undergo a certification course?

What knowledge and tools do they usually use in their job?

Are there any specific applications and tools they use daily? Getting to know about the products they like to use can help you understand how your products will fare.

Questions about their issues or challenges

What are their biggest obstacles?

You are in business because the products or services you offer a help solve a problem for your target customers. If that problem wasn't solved, how would it affect their daily lives? Try to elucidate how the said problem makes your target audience feel. For instance, if your business deals in personal taxation software, which is directly sold to the customers, one of the customer personas you create might be a first-time taxpayer. What are the different challenges a first-time taxpayer might face? Make a list of all the likely hurdles they might run into and offer an explanation as to how your business can solve the same.

Questions about their buying habits

Ask them to describe their recent purchase.

What were their reasons for making the purchase? What evaluation process did they undergo while selecting the product to buy? How was their buying experience? Would they buy a similar product in the future? Is there anything they would want to change about the buying process?

Do they search for products or services online before making a purchase?

Does your customer persona spend any time online to look for products and services and to compare the prices? If yes, then what are the different online portals they refer to? Do you ask others for their opinions before buying a product or availing a service?

Do they spend any time online on social media sites?

What is their go-to social media networking site? How frequently do they check their social media accounts, and what are their favorite pages? Do they read any online magazines and blogs?

Create Your Own Buyer Persona

Now, it is time to create customer personas for your business. Here are some questions you can ask while creating customer personas.

- Describe their personal demographics.
- Describe their educational background.
- Describe their career path.
- Where do they work and what is their job profile?
- What does a typical day in their life look like?
- What are their unique skills?
- Does their job require any special skills?
- What are their biggest challenges?
- What are their goals?
- What are their fears?
- What triggers them?
- What encourages them to buy?
- What is their buying behavior?
- Are there any obstacles they face?
- What is their online behavior?

- What platforms or apps do they frequently use?
- Do they have any brand affinities? If yes, then what are their favorite brands?
- What are they looking for?
- What will make their life easier?

Once you complete this exercise and work out all these details, you will have a thorough idea of what your target customers are looking for. You can also go through the different stock photos available online and find one that fits your customer profile perfectly. It helps provide a clear image of your ideal customer for your business. Once you have a customer persona in place, it becomes easier to concentrate on your marketing efforts and make the necessary changes.

Chapter 2: Sales Funnel

About a Sales Funnel

A sales funnel is a marketing term that's used to describe the journey that a potential customer goes through on their way to making a purchase. There are various steps in a sales funnel which are generally referred to as the top, middle, and the bottom of the sales funnel. The names of these steps differ depending on the model of the sales funnel. The pain of missing out on a sale is something that all business owners are familiar with. At times, even after a couple of weeks of sales pitches, demos, conversations, and chatter, a prospective customer can drop out of a sales funnel without making a purchase. This is quite common. However, the chances of this can be reduced drastically by using the proper sales funnel. The sales funnels used by small businesses are like sieves with gaps left by barely held together spreadsheets, sticky notes, forgotten follow-up calls, and missed appointments.

There is a simple way to fix it, and that's by developing a good sales funnel that doesn't leave any holes. The different steps involved in the sales funnel help filter out people so that only the interested customers are in the funnel. As you go along, the process keeps narrowing the field of interested parties, and you will be left with a funnel-like structure.

The first phase of the sales funnel is referred to as the "awareness" stage. This is the phase wherein people become aware of your business and the products or services you offer for the first time. They might have heard about your business from others, through social media, or even advertisements. The reasons for why and how such people move further along the sales funnel solely depends on your sales and marketing efforts. The leads formed along the middle and lower stages of a sales funnel are those that you must concentrate the most on since it consists of individuals who have moved from the phase of awareness to that of "interest."

Now you will be able to see the importance of a sales funnel. Even if the leads are quite good, they can easily slip out of the funnel if you don't nurture them carefully. The best way to minimize or even prevent such loss is by having a clear idea of all the steps that you must include in the sales process. You will learn about the different steps involved in the subsequent sections.

Sales funnels are necessary for all those businesses which depend on interaction and engagement with prospects for closing sales. Their sales process might be complicated, or they might merely be dealing with high-ticket items that require consideration and deliberation by the customer before making a purchase. All businesses which have either B2B or B2C models can use sales funnels. Businesses, as well as sales professionals, can use sales funnels. Sales managers and professionals tend to use sales funnels to plan their sales activities to improve their leads from the beginning of the funnel to its end. Marketing managers tend to use sales funnels for creating leads, which are in alignment with the business's brand and for establishing good customer relations for a higher rate of conversions. Business owners use sales funnels for a similar reason as marketing managers.

Different Stages

The stages in a sales funnel include all the steps that a prospective customer goes through, and they determine how close the lead is to being converted into a customer. There are five stages in a sales funnel, and they can be easily customized according to your business needs. The different stages are as follows.

Awareness

The first stage is that of awareness. This stage refers to the first time when your prospective customers become aware of your business, products or services, and your brand. It is primarily an introductory phase wherein they learn about who you are, what your business is about, and the factors which make your business unique.

Discovery

Once the prospective customer's interest is piqued, they move into the next stage, and that's discovery. Now, the prospects are quite curious about your business and the products you offer. The prospects are quite eager to learn more about your business. In this stage, you will need to provide them with valuable and educational content which is related to a problem or a need your prospects have. This stage takes place when you are qualifying a lead and are defining their needs.

Evaluation

Now, your prospects are armed with all the information they need. Once they have all the information they need, it is time for them to evaluate your business along with the products or services you offer. They will also be actively seeking out other options and comparing the different alternatives to see how you fare. At this stage, it is time to send your initial proposal or even a quote to them.

Purchase

In this stage, the prospect has decided to make a purchase, but the deal hasn't been finalized yet. They intend to buy but will want a proposal or a quote from your business regarding the price they are willing to pay. In this stage, you can negotiate the terms or even finalize the proposal. Once this is done, the prospect is ready to take the next step and seal the deal. Voila! Now your business has acquired a new customer. This is a sweet step, and it gives you a chance to ask the customer for referrals.

Loyalty

If your business deals with such products or services which will be delivered over a period, then it gives you a chance to offer other products which the customer might need. Essentially, it gives you the time to identify other needs and make any additional sales. However, if it is a one-time purchase, then this is the opportunity your business needs to establish loyalty and ensure repeat business. Most small business owners tend to combine the purchase and loyalty stages of a sales funnel and place them as a single stage.

Importance of a Sales Funnel

Selecting a marketing strategy

Most often, small businesses tend to blow their marketing budget on strategies that only yield minimal results. To avoid this, you need a sales funnel. It helps you understand the different marketing strategies and tools your business model needs to ensure success. For instance, if most of the prospects of your business are in the awareness stage, then you need to develop a marketing campaign that focuses on moving them along to the next stages of the sales funnel. Some marketers tend to focus on those leads which are in the decision phase of the sales funnel. If the marketers know which stage the leads are in, then they can take the necessary steps to move them further along the sales funnel and drive them to the goal-making a purchase.

Relate to the customer

Did you know that most businesses tend to operate in their own jargon? At times, the way the business describes its products, the content produced, or the way you talk to your clients helps move them further along the sales funnel. Once you can identify the stage within which most of the leads are present, then you can readily change the tone and content of your copy and create well-targeted content which will help convince the leads to move along the sales funnel.

Generating more sales

When you can select a good marketing strategy, the right marketing tools, and are aware of how you can relate to your prospects, you can drive more prospects toward the purchase stage. If you have good sales funnel management in place, then you will be able to generate more sales in the long run for your business. The fundamental principle of a sales funnel is to learn how you can methodically draw the outcome you desire from your prospects.

Standout from other entrepreneurs

A common problem faced by entrepreneurs, especially the

newbies, is the lack of proper direction. They might have a ton of great ideas, but they aren't capable of executing those ideas since they don't have a system in place to implement them for making sales. Having a thorough understanding of a sales funnel gives you a competitive advantage over all those present in your chosen niche.

Grow your business

When it comes to business, there is no such thing as a perfect business model. A lot of those overnight success stories you hear about in business don't necessarily happen overnight. A sales funnel can help you obtain the essential feedback about all those marketing strategies which can help improve your sales. Not just your sales, but it also paves the way for developing and strengthening customer relations and loyalty. A combination of all these things helps in the growth of your business. For instance, you might have noticed that a lot of your leads who are keen on making a purchase don't finalize the deal because of the product pricing. When you have such insights available, you can easily use them to restructure your product pricing model and choose a price that works favorably for the business as well as the customers.

A sales funnel is certainly an integral part of a successful marketing strategy. As you begin to identify each potential customer's stage in the sales funnel, you will start to become adept at generating and converting those leads to improve your sales.

Possible Leaks to Plug

Once you are aware of the different stages you want to include in your sales funnel, it is time to analyze where you end up losing your potential customers. As a small business owner, you must sit down with your team at work and ask the following questions.

- What are the different obstructions in the sales process?
- Where does your business lose track of prospective customers?
- Are there any positive triggers that can help increase sales?

Take a close look at the different cracks present in the funnel, then fix them. There are three primary causes of such leaks, and they are as follows.

Moving over the "no's"

When it comes to sales, a "no" usually means "maybe not now, but later." For instance, a usual objection for a business that is selling customer relationship management software is, "I don't have the necessary time to get all the content finalized for making the platform useful." An objection like this means the prospect is interested in the product being offered but isn't ready at the moment. While working on leads, it might be rather tempting to ignore such leads and move onto a more viable one.

Instead of throwing away the prospects the moment they raise an objection to purchasing, you need to find a solution. You can develop an automated email follow-up system that addresses their objections directly. Whenever you encounter such an objection in the future, you can merely send the predesigned information to the prospect. It will certainly take some time and effort to convince the prospect to become a customer, but it will eventually happen if you are persistent.

Make a note of all the common objections you receive from your leads and think of how you can turn them around with useful content and an automated follow-up system. Identify the stages in your sales funnel wherein you are easily and quickly dismissing any prospects and work to fix the leak.

Failure to follow-up

Are you following up with your prospects as often as you should be? Well, a majority of businesses usually fail to follow up with their prospective customers. According to the National Sales Executive Association, about 80% of the sales are finalized between the fifth and the twelfth contact a business makes with the prospective customers. So, that's a lot of ground to cover. The challenge is quite simple - do you need to call new leads, or do you need to follow up with an existing lead for the fifth time? Persistence might feel like nothing more than a waste of time, but that's not what the data suggests. Automating your sales funnel is a good idea for small businesses. Instead of debating about whether to call existing or new leads, an automated funnel will help you do both. All your leads will receive regular, consistent, and friendly emails at all stages of the sales funnel. Take some time and analyze the last twenty leads you had and count the number of times you had to contact to enable conversion. This will help you arrive at an average number of follow-ups you will need to do to convert a lead into a customer successfully.

Being too slow

The data provided by the National Sales Executive Association also shows that a new lead is nine times more likely to convert provided you go ahead with a follow-up within the first five minutes of their expressing interest. Waiting for over thirty minutes brings this number down, and the lead is twenty-one times less likely to convert into a paying customer. You might be thinking it sounds impossible to be able to contact that lead within the first five minutes of them expressing their interest in your products. This is where an automated sales funnel management system comes into the picture. You must set up the system such that it generates an automatic response as you desire, which will be immediately sent to the prospects as soon as they express any interest. As the lead moves further along the sales funnel, you can program the automation system to send personalized emails that are in sync with the lead's movement in the sales funnel. Take some time and analyze the time that's usually taken to respond to a new prospect. Once you have this number, you can draft a mass personalized email that can be sent to all prospects readily.

Value Ladder

Imagine if there was a means you could use to maximize the purchases made by every customer of your business. Yes, this can be done, with the help of a value ladder. If you have never heard of this term, then it is quite likely that you have been letting go of several sales opportunities for your business. It can be rather tricky to precisely understand how much a customer is willing to spend without asking them this question directly. Usually, a lot of buyers tend to underestimate or even lie about their buying power, and most leads don't convert when they are faced with an entry price point.

Let us look at what a business without a value ladder looks like. For instance, you have three possible leads who want to purchase your product. The three potential customers are Customer A, B, and C, and each of them has $20, $50, and $250 to spend. Your business offers a variety of products between the price range of $30 to $70. Customer A cannot afford to purchase anything from your business and will therefore not spend anything. B is capable of spending $50 and might, therefore, ask for a discounted or a lower-priced product that will fulfill his need. If he gets a good deal, he will spend $50. Customer C will realize that even the most costly item available is well within his budget and will spend $70 readily. So, the total sales made add up to $120. If you had a value ladder, you would have been able to earn $320 from the sales. So, by adding a value ladder to your business, you can work on maximizing the purchases made by the customers.

Now you are aware of what happens to businesses that don't have a value ladder. So, what does a value ladder mean? It refers to a wide range of products or services listed in ascending order of their price from the lowest value offer to the highest-priced or premium category products. The customers are guided to make their way through each of these stages of the value ladder and maximize their spending. To fully understand the usefulness of a value ladder, let us go back to the previous example. You once again have three prospects, but your business operates quite differently in this situation. Instead of giving the prospects a price range of all the products available, you give them a free service or an extremely low-price product. Once this is done, you make an offer to the next tier of the value ladder in place. This will go on indefinitely - the best value ladders either have no endpoint or end such that it increases the chances of a repeat purchase.

In this case, the business starts its value ladder from $0, then adds products along with the price range of $5, $15, $30, $75,

$125, $250, $500, and so on. So, what will happen to the three customers now? Customer A will accept the first free product, and this might go on to impress him so much that he goes on to spend his money on the next two tiers, too. The same happens to customer B, and he spends his budget on three tiers of products. Customer C walks away buying four tiers in the ladder - $5, $15, $30, $75 and spends $125. He is so happy that he got more than what he had bargained for and therefore, ends up spending the rest of his budget, too. Essentially, you end up with $320 in the form of sales, and your business has managed to maximize the customer's purchasing power.

The structure, along with the staging of the value ladder, is incredibly important in determining its success. In the previous example, the value ladder is structured rather perfectly, and this seldom happens in reality. Before you can start planning the different tiers of the ladder, you must understand one thing- the very first offer cannot be a sales meeting or a consultation. The first offer needs to be appealing and irresistible; it must be something that the leads usually pay for and are now getting for free. When you do this, the prospect is given a chance to see the value that your business is offering. This tends to influence and goad them into purchasing from your business.

Essentially, the free or low-cost offer is the bait you are setting. It helps increase the number of leads who step onto the value ladder. Not just that, it also helps increase awareness about your business, and you can create a list of potential customers, too. The tier after this one needs to be priced such that it covers the costs of the previous offer along with the current one. For instance, if the first offer costs you $2 and the second one costs $3, then the second offer needs to be priced at $5. Until now, you have done nothing but break even. However, you have managed to provide two products to your customers at an incredibly competitive price, and the value they derive from your business has them hooked. Once you breakeven, every offer from now on will help your business earn a profit. You must ensure that the customers don't skip any stages because a value ladder helps maximize the customer's purchases only if they proceed in the desired order of spending.

Value ladders are quite common, and a lot of industries use different types of value ladders to attract and retain customers. For instance, a business selling snacks might offer the first box of snacks for free. The next step consists of offering a discount coupon for single-use at a supermarket. The third tier of the ladder consists of purchasing the product at its full price. The fourth tier consists of subscribing to receive the product once every month, and the final tier consists of upgrading this service to increase the frequency of the deliveries.

Chapter 3: Customer Journey

How do you determine what the customers want? What happens when you believe that you are offering your customers all that they need, but they end up shopping at your competitor's business? The simplest means of understanding what your business is missing is to go through a customer journey.

So, what is a customer journey? It is essentially a roadmap that shows you how a customer tends to become aware of your business, and the interactions they have with your business and your brand. Instead of merely concentrating on one part of the customer experience, the customer journey is a documentation of the entire experience of being a customer. That does sound like a lot to cover, but understanding the customer journey is not tricky as long as you stay organized.

By understanding the customer journey, you can help nurture and enhance the experience your customers have. Usually, whenever a customer purchases a product or uses a service, they expect that a pleasant feeling of happiness or satisfaction will accompany their purchase. This sense of satisfaction that people experience when they find something they want, and finally purchase and enjoy it is something a business must not discount. Customers tend to pay attention to how easy or problematic their entire experience was. If they have a positive experience, it is quite likely that they will either repeat their purchase or even tell others about the wonderful experience they have had. To get a better understanding of the customer journey, it is time to think about it from a customer's perspective. Whenever there is any scope to learn or explore, you will notice the word "(ping)" mentioned.

For instance, your potential customer is out shopping, and she sees your store along with all the signage (ping). She walks into the store and observes the store layout (ping). One of your employees goes to greet her (ping) and offers her assistance (ping). The employee is quite friendly (ping) as well as knowledgeable (ping) about the store and helps the customer choose something that meets her requirements. The potential customer is now ready to make a purchase, and she is assured that even if she does change her mind about the purchase, she can return the same within a week without any questions asked (ping). In the evening, your customer posts a picture of her new purchase on Facebook and also mentions your business (ping). She even recommends your store to all her followers on yelp.com (ping) because of the wonderful experience she had at the store. Now, you have acquired a loyal customer. After a couple of weeks, you send her a promotional email (ping) which gives her an exclusive discount (ping), and it reminds her of the pleasant feelings she had at the store and the values your business promotes (ping). This is just one instance. However, if you don't pay any attention and don't try to understand the mindset of your customers, then you will not be able to do your business any justice. If the potential customer has an unpleasant experience, then she might not even make a purchase. Or if her shopping experience was frustrating, then she will end up associating all those negative emotions with your brand and business. For instance, if she had to deal with rude employees, unhelpful employees, or couldn't find the product she was looking for, they all amount to a negative experience. If she ever has to buy the same product again, she will opt to go to your competitor's store because of the frustrating experience she had at your store. She might even convey her negative experience to others, and this can discourage other potential customers from doing business with you. You can certainly see the importance of paying attention to the customer journey now!

Benefits It Offers

Understanding the perspective of the customer is quite important when you want to understand the experience they have with your business. This is the primary reason why businesses concentrate on mapping out the customer journey for studying the customer experience and learning the places where there is scope for improvement. By analyzing the quantitative data and taking into account the feedback from customers and employees, a business can develop comprehensive maps that reflect the motivation and sentiments a potential customer undergoes on their way to becoming loyal customers. Here are all the different benefits of understanding the customer journey.

Understand underlying emotions

As potential customers go from one point to another, a map shows how easily they can do this. For instance, is your prospect able to get in touch with an agent quickly by using the IVR menu? Can the prospect switch from the business's social media page to the official page easily? What is the level of customer satisfaction after the contact is made? The answers to all these questions show how the prospect feels about every step of the journey and helps businesses improve their practices by identifying which ones tend to cause ambiguity or even frustration. Businesses can also learn about the different aspects of their workings which satisfy their customers and can divert their time and resources on perfecting such practices.

Identify any gaps

Mapping the customer's journey can also help identify any gaps which exist in the customer service you provide. For instance, you may be able to identify channels that are frequently used by the customer but are understaffed, which results in frustration on the part of the customer. Similarly, switching from the desktop to the mobile versions of your website might not be fully optimized, and this causes a communication gap. Any problems regarding the lines of communication between employees can also be discovered if the employees aren't able to receive the necessary support they need during customer interactions. So, mapping the customer journey helps you identify any gaps that exist in your internal routes of communication in your business.

Reduction of costs

Businesses that use customer journey analysis can also reduce their costs according to the research conducted by the Aberdeen Group. It is reported that brands which map customer journey can experience ten times the improvement in their costs of customer service when compared to those brands that don't. Also, an increase in the word of mouth publicity helps decrease customer turnover, which in turn reduces the costs involved in acquiring new customers for the business.

Better sales

If you are well versed in the customer journey and are aware of the different things you can do to make the customer experience better, it increases your sales. In fact, it helps increase the revenue generated from any upselling and cross-selling efforts of your business. Also, it helps in improving your marketing efforts, which in turn improves the ROI on your marketing practices. So, you can optimize your sales as well as marketing strategies with the help of the customer journey map.

Improved levels of satisfaction

As the customers get the experience they desire, the level of customer satisfaction will naturally increase. Also, when you work on improving the communication problems within the business, it improves employee satisfaction, too. When you are aware of what you want the employees to do, it becomes easier to explain the same to them. This improves their understanding of what their job is and how they can help attain the business objectives along the way.

Sales Funnel vs. Customer Journey

There is a difference between a sales funnel and a customer journey. A sales funnel suggests that the top of the funnel consists of prospects who are mildly interested in your business and are merely looking at all that you offer. The lower they move along in the funnel, the more the event of conversion becomes a certainty. This is a rather simple way to look at the process of marketing and sales. The customer journey helps map out all the possible touchpoints a customer goes through while moving along the sales funnel. Here is an example of what a customer journey will look like in the digital world.

The prospect comes across a billboard of digital marketing or perhaps a display campaign on YouTube while going through something else online. It is quite likely that the prospect was targeted because of their usual behavior or even because of the demographic. For instance, a woman in her late twenties might be an ideal target for a campaign or ads for pregnancy tests and other fertility products based solely on her age and gender.

Once the prospect has visited the website of the business, it shows their interest. The prospect might have downloaded a brochure, surfed through a couple of pages, or even requested a quote. Then it is time for remarketing the content on other channels like any of the social media platforms and news websites.

Then comes the moment when the prospect will likely engage in content marketing of your business. For instance, the prospect might view videos about a specific product she wishes to purchase. This is the stage wherein a prospect will probably search for your business online and click on the ads displayed by the search engine.

When the prospect is prepped to buy, she will probably directly search for the brand online, locate the store, or even order the product online.

After the action is taken, it is time to leave a review for the product. A stage that was traditionally overlooked in a sales funnel is the post-action phase. This is the stage where the customer shares their experience of doing business with your brand and posts the same information on social media or even passes it on through word of mouth. This is an important stage because this stage has the power of generating referrals for your business.

Steps to Follow

Customer Persona

The first thing to do before you can start mapping out the customer journey is to understand your customers. The best way to understand your customers is by creating buyer personas. You need to step into the shoes of your potential customers and understand their behavior, along with their likes and dislikes as well as their wants and needs. Yes, all individuals are different, but a buyer persona gives you the insight you need to map out the customer journey. If you have not yet developed customer personas, then you must do that right away. Follow the steps given in the previous chapters to come up with detailed customer personas for your business.

While you do this, you must remember that you need to have several buyer personas ready. The prospects at different stages of the sales cycle will act, think, and interact differently with your business. So, it is prudent to differentiate between those prospects who have been doing their market research for a while and are keen on purchasing from someone who has recently become interested in your business.

Understanding the customer's goals

Once you have curated the buyer personas, you must start digging around a little and try to understand the goals each customer hopes to achieve through their journey. Take some time and think about the ultimate goal of the customer in each phase. For instance, the goal of a customer might be to analyze the different options available in the market, make sure that they aren't overspending, or even find reassurance that they are making the right decision.

A simple way to go about this is to identify the different paths your prospects might take on your business website. If your prospect is a pre-existing customer, it is quite likely that the first step is to log in to their member profile on the website. Other activities you can concentrate on include searching for products, browsing the menu, comparing the products, and so on. Once you make a complete list of all the activities a customer might perform, you must make a note of the different touchpoints and goals related to each of the touchpoints.

Once you have an idea of touchpoints, you must determine the different goals a customer has at each of those touchpoints. By mapping out the goals, it becomes easier to understand whether your business has been meeting such goals or not.

Here are a couple of different things you can do to understand the goals of your customers.

- Survey or interview different groups of customers
- Go through the customer support transcripts and emails
- Identify the different customer questions in each of the phases
- Obtain feedback for user testing
- Talk to the customers

Mapping out the touchpoints

A touchpoint refers to all those times wherein a prospect comes into contact with your business before, during, or even after making the purchase. It also includes different instances that can take place online or offline, via marketing, in person, or even over the phone. Some touchpoints tend to have a greater impact than others. For instance, a poor check-in experience at a hotel can taint the way the customer views their entire stay. You must consider all the possible touchpoints which take place between your prospects and the business. By doing this, you can ensure that you don't miss out on any chances of listening to customer feedback and making the necessary changes that can improve the customer experience.

So, how can you identify the different touchpoints? Since there are several ways in which customers experience your business, the idea of making a list of all possible touchpoints can seem overwhelming. However, by placing yourself in your customer's shoes, it becomes easier to go along their journey. Here is a simple exercise you can use while making a list of the touchpoints.

"Where can I go (and how can I get there) when..."

... I have an (issue with which your business or product remedies)?

... I find the product or business which solves my issues?

... I make up my mind about making a purchase?

... I come across the business after making the purchase?

By answering these questions, you will have a list of all the touchpoints. Another way to go about this is to simply ask the customers about their experience with your business or even include the questions mentioned above in the customer feedback or survey.

If you have set up Google Analytics for your website, then there are two reports which will come in handy. The first one is the behavior flow report, which shows the movement of a customer through your website, one step at a time. It helps you understand the way a customer behaves, the different paths they take while going through the website, and the different sources, mediums, or campaigns they come from. Apart from this, it also helps you make a note of any pain points on your website that the prospects struggle with. The second report is the goal flow report. This report shows the path your prospects take to complete your goal of conversion. It helps show how the prospects navigate the sales funnels and if there are any points which have a high drop-off rate that must be addressed.

Identify the pain points

At this stage, it is time to put all your qualitative and quantitative data together and try to look at the big picture. You essentially need to identify any potential roadblocks, or any pain points your customer experiences on their journey. You must also make a list of all those things you are doing well right now and must think of ways to take things up a notch. To do this, you must interview your customers as well as your employees who deal with customers. Here are certain questions you can include in the interview.

- Are the prospects able to achieve their goals on the business website?
- What are the main spots which seem to be causing frustration and friction?
- Are the prospects abandoning their purchase at any stage? If yes, then why?

Once you are aware of the different pain points and obstructions, make a note of them on the customer journey map.

Fix the roadblocks

Here are questions you can ask yourself while trying to fix the roadblocks: What are the changes to be made and what must be corrected? Do I need to do away with everything and start from scratch once again? Or can I make a couple of simple changes that can improve the overall customer experience?

For instance, if you notice that customers tend to complain that the signup process on your website is complicated, then it is probably a good idea to revamp it and make it simpler for your customers. Once you identify the roadblocks that exist, take a look at the big picture. Understand that the goal is to optimize each touchpoint, not for the sake of optimizing it, but because it will help move the customers further along the sales funnel and encourage them to convert. After all, your goal is to increase conversions. So, remember that all the changes that you make must help you attain your goal.

Time to update

Your job doesn't come to an end after you create the customer journey map. It is not a one-time activity. You need to keep updating it constantly to keep up with the constantly changing and ever-evolving customer behavior. You will need to keep testing, updating it, and improving it at least twice a year if you want it to be effective.

Things to Keep in Mind

There are different customer touchpoints you must concentrate on while mapping out the customer journey. The customer touchpoints are all the times when the customer comes in contact with your brand or business. There will be different touchpoints like the ads you publish or your website with which your customers will interact. Once you assume the customer mindset, you can start listing out the potential touchpoints like the reviews on social media, your business website, the customer service team, and even feedback and follow-up surveys. While analyzing the different stages and mapping out the customer journey, you must keep the following in mind.

- Once you figure out all the stages of the customer journey, you must think about what the customer does at each of these stages. You must think about the specific actions the customer takes along the way.

- What are the things which encourage or prevent the customer from moving onto the next stage? Are there any motivations or emotions which the customer experiences at each stage?

- Are there any points where the customers get stuck? Do the customers have any questions and do they find it difficult to find answers to such questions? Do they experience any uncertainties which prompt them to give up and go to your competitors? Are there any inherent complications in the products you offer, and can you do anything to remove such complications?

- Are there any obstacles the customers face in each of the stages of their journey? Is it related to the cost of the products or services involved? Are there any troubles with the return policy? Thinking about all these things will help you understand the possible reasons why a customer drops out of the sales cycle without making a purchase.

You can use diagrams to map out the customer journey or even create a list of different scenarios the customer goes through at each stage. You can create customer feedback surveys to understand what changes they would like. Please remember that the experience and the journey of customers tend to vary, and some might even skip a couple of stages altogether in their journey. This is precisely why you must walk through different scenarios and talk to your customers to get a better understanding of their journey.

By following the steps given in this section, you can easily map out the customer journey. Now, here is a small assignment for you: Keeping the information given in this section in mind, take some time and start mapping out the customer journey for your business.

Chapter 4: First Stop- The Awareness Phase

The first stage of the sales funnel is the awareness stage. In this stage, the prospect has a need or an issue that must be solved. They might not know what is required to solve their issues or satisfy their needs. They might not know much about the need, problem, or opportunity available at this stage. Their research for the solution at this stage consists of using phrases or words to describe their problem, the relief they are seeking, or the means to fulfill their needs. The fact that this stage represents an opportunity for your prospect is seldom spoken about. If you are a B2B company and your target customer has grown enough to reap the benefits of the solution you offer, then the said customer is displaying the symptoms. You must be able to identify and name them. If your prospect has witnessed business growth and your solution can help them grow further and give them a competitive advantage, then you must know the symptoms they experience to create content which will resonate with them at this stage.

When your prospects are in this first stage of the sales funnel, they usually search to understand the negative symptoms they experience. All of these prospects tend to have a problem that must be resolved. Your prospects are usually searching online for:

1. Any symptoms which match their own
2. A better understanding of their problem
3. The name of their problem
4. The different available solutions

So, what do the prospects look for at this stage? Before you can start creating content to attract your potential clients, you must understand what they look for at this stage. At this point, they are merely looking for a better understanding of their problem. They want information and are actively seeking knowledge about the same. The prospects aren't thinking about your business, brand, or even your products at the moment. Now is not the stage to start promoting your product to them.

The content which you must create for this stage of the sales funnel must be essentially educational. It needs to add value to the prospects' lives and must help them understand their needs better. The relationship you want to establish with your customers at this point purely depends on the quality and usefulness of the content you provide them. The better the content is, the more they will want to read about other posts, come back for more, and perhaps share your content. The purpose of the content at this stage is to ensure that your prospects stick around and go through more content. Navigating your website at this stage will help them move along their customer journey.

At this point, the call to action for any business must be to offer them good quality and helpful content to read. This is not the time to offer them any discounts. Don't place any trial offers at the end of the articles you publish. The prospect isn't ready to buy, not yet. Exposing the prospects to unnecessary sales pitches will ruin any chances of selling that you had. Instead, it is time to invite them to go through more of your content. By exposing the prospects to good content, you can easily keep them around.

It is quintessential to make a note of the different sources which generate prospects who are in the awareness stage. The different sources include results on search engines, social media networking sites like Facebook, Instagram, Twitter, and the like, online forums and groups, guest postings, and backlinks. Understanding where the traffic originates from is quite important since it helps you optimize your marketing strategies. Most of these channels are important in almost all the stages of the sales funnel, but optimizing them for the awareness stage is a good idea if you want to increase the number of prospects of your business.

The success of your marketing campaigns will depend on your understanding of buyer personas and your ability to leverage them. It is quintessential that you have well-thought-out buyer personas for all types of customers your business can expect. You cannot develop magnetizing and appealing content for the awareness phase of the sales funnel if you haven't developed the buyer personas yet. Once you have the buyer personas, then you can start defining the journey that they will take as they try to resolve their issues and make their way toward a buying decision. When you detail and define the buyer persona and map out the customer journey, you will effectively be taking all sorts of the guesswork out of the equation and can concentrate on developing effective content.

All prospects start in the awareness phase. However, it isn't necessary that every buyer who visits your website is present in the awareness stage. This is the stage wherein the buyer persona begins to attain a greater awareness of their issue. The prospect is experiencing pain, challenges, or maybe an opportunity they never had before. The prospects have realized that something is amiss or that they have attained such growth or success that it creates the need for an answer. The prospect's goal at this stage is to understand their problem and find a solution. If you are interested in marketing effectively to all those prospects who are in the awareness stage, then you need to understand their mindset. Try to understand the problem they are facing and the motivations or emotions which encourage them to solve their problem. By mapping out the customer journey of the buyer personas you have developed, you will be able to get some clarity and insight about the buyer's mindset.

What kind of content are the buyers in the awareness phase looking for? The kind of content prospects in this phase will be looking for can be divided into three categories- a list of different symptoms, a description of issues, and information that's specific to the industry. As mentioned, the buyers in the awareness phase know they are facing a problem. They are asking questions about the symptoms which are similar to the ones they are experiencing. What they don't understand is that the symptoms they are experiencing can affect other aspects of their business, too. So, you will need to draw these people to your website with content that lists their symptoms. You must help them and inspire trust as you are trying to help them understand their problems.

You must create content such that it provides details and gives a list of all the issues they are facing and the potential problems they will face in the future if the issue is left unresolved. It is quintessential that you create content which contains what they are aware of because most of their research will be based on what they know. They will be looking up their symptoms in the online search engines. Your click-through rates will increase if the content you provide is not just relevant and of good quality but is well-optimized, too. The content must provide them with insight into their problems.

You can also provide them with lists, white papers, eBooks, and also content which provide industry-specific data, research, and reports about their situation. The content you make available must not only address their pain and symptoms, but it must also include the different options others followed and how it helped eliminate their problems.

By including the experiences of other clients or by providing customer testimonials, you can convince the prospects to move onto the next stage of the sales funnel. Buyers are actively seeking information which points them toward a solution.

What are the pages that the buyers in the awareness phase usually visit? The buyers are only seeking educational content instead of sales pitches. If you have a blog, then the buyers will thoroughly review it in this phase. Ensure that you also include links to any other industry-related articles and data in these blogs. Your goal at this stage is to try to establish yourself as an industry expert. Only if the prospects think that you are an industry expert will they want to learn more about your business and products in the next stages. They are actively looking for content with high integrity, which will enable them to diagnose their problems. So, you must provide them with informative and well-written articles that offer quality content and are easy to understand. They need to be able to draw accurate conclusions from the information you give them. Only when this is done will they be willing to move along their customer journey and enter the next step in the sales funnel you have designed. Different social media sites will help the prospects in the awareness phase identify with others who have the same concerns. This allows them to connect with others who can give them helpful advice. As an industry expert, you must always have your prospect's best interest in mind. Your content along with other advice they receive from you must convince them that you are an industry expert. You need to carefully nurture your leads in this phase and help them move on. You will notice that it gets easier to convert a visitor to a lead and then into a customer if you provide them with the necessary content.

Since the prospects are looking for content that's trustworthy and informative, the format of content you use must convey the same. The best formats for content in this stage include reports of research, analysis of research, white papers, eBooks, and educational webinars and blog posts.

The landing pages you create must have certain elements that need to appeal to your target audience. Remember that the content you are creating must appeal to the specific buyer personas you have created. The landing pages need to contain an offer, an explanatory paragraph, several bulleted statements, form fields, along with a call-to-action or CTA button. The offer you present must be in a format that will appeal to your target audience. Try to create aesthetically pleasing three-dimensional images and titles or subtitles that are compelling and interesting. The offer must be accompanied by an explanatory paragraph that gives a piece of succinct and value-laden information which will make it difficult for the viewer to refuse. The things you are offering or the solutions you propose must be presented in bulleted statements which give a brief overview of how the prospect's problems can be solved.

The call-to-action or CTA button you place on the landing page needs to be quite compelling. Design it such that it inspires the viewer to take the action you desire. You can include a compelling image showing the outcome to be delivered by the content below the CTA button. The text included in the CTA must be more than a generic word like "submit," and must include something specific like "Click here to resolve your issue immediately." You also need to place form fields for capturing the information about the leads who visit the landing page. In the awareness stage, you must not request a lot of information from the leads - try to limit it to their email address. If you feel that having their first name along with their email address is important to provide them useful content, only then should you ask for both.

Nurture Them

Once you have the prospects in the awareness stage, you are required to nurture them so that they move along the sales funnel. How can a business nurture their prospects? You must understand that most of the prospects at this stage are rather overwhelmed. So, you need to nurture them so that they proceed forward gently. If you do this well, your prospects will certainly appreciate the effort you've put into providing them with educational material. The way you nurture your leads in this stage can give you a competitive edge over others in the industry. Here are a couple of things you can do to nurture your buyers:

The first thing you must do is ensure that you create trust. You must assure the buyers that you will be with them throughout the buying process. Some prospects need a little reassurance from time to time. The best way to do this is by showing the prospects that you only have their best interests in mind and that you will help them answer their questions and solve their problems or issue.

You need to create a reputation for yourself as an expert in the industry. The simplest means to do this is by sending them research, case studies, or any other high-quality and high-value content you come across. The information that you provide them with can influence their decision to buy or do business with you.

You must ensure that there are necessary channels in place that will ensure that relevant communication takes place regardless of the stage the prospect is in the sales funnel. You can maintain a good customer relationship through regular emails and phone contact. Your prospect will feel more comfortable in doing business with you and will warm up to your business if you nurture them.

Content for This Stage

Now, this is the most exciting part of this stage. By now, you must have an idea of what your prospects are expecting. You are also aware of the fact that you must nurture their interest as well as expectations. There is one thing that is left to decide if you want to win them over, and that's selecting the right topics for the content you create. If you wish to stand apart from your competitors in your niche, you will need to select the right topics. You might have probably established an editorial calendar for the rest of the month. It might work for you. However, if you are interested in nurturing your prospects at this stage and encourage them to move ahead, then you need to work on the topics you wish to develop content on. There are three simple steps you must follow to ensure that you come up with the right content for this stage, and they are as follows.

1. The first thing you need to do is identify the problem or need your product or business is fulfilling. A lot of people tend to create unfocused or extremely broad content for the awareness phase, and that's a mistake you must avoid. The content you create must not only be valuable, interesting, and educational, but it must also be well-targeted. If you wish for your prospects to regard you as an authority, then you must refocus and learn to be specific. You must concentrate on creating content around the problem or need your business can help the prospects solve. Doing this will enable your business to seem like an expert in your chosen niche. Also, by creating content that's focused on the need you

solve, it makes it easier for prospects to move along the sales funnel rather quickly. For instance, if a business is selling custom-made shoes for those with narrow feet, then the need they are solving is quite specific. So, the content that the business needs to create during the awareness phase will be based on the problems those with narrow feet face and how the same can be resolved. Take some time and make a list of all the core issues your business is solving, and you can develop content for them.

2. The second thing you need to do is spend some time researching all the trending topics associated with that problem. You can use Google or a tool like Buzzsumo. It will help you understand all the different topics that your prospects find exciting. Not just that, it will help you shortlist all those topics that will click with your ideal audience. Try to identify the top-performing content for those topics and strive to create better content.

3. The final step is to conduct a keyword search using tools like Moz Keyword explorer or Google. It is quite important that you make a list of all the popular and trending keywords related to the issue. Doing this will give you an idea about what others are looking for while in the awareness stage. Keep these keywords and trending topics in mind when you start creating

content. Also, you must ensure that the content you are creating is optimized for search engines and contains all the important keywords.

Use Social Media to Build Awareness

Using social media to build awareness is the best way in which you can nurture the prospects in the awareness phase. Here are certain techniques you can use to build your brand's awareness online.

- The first thing you can do is start encouraging social sharing. You must encourage your fans and followers on social media to share your posts. The way they share your posts will depend on the platform you use. A retweet, a shared post on Instagram, or even a repin on Pinterest can help spread awareness about your brand to a new audience.

- Everyone likes to win contests. So, leverage social media for creating contests that will spread awareness about your business. Creating a simple contest wherein the participants stand to win a free product for the best caption they come up with for your posts is a good idea. This is a good means to engage your audience and introduce your business to a newer audience.

- Creating fresh and valuable content will automatically

increase your popularity with your followers. The content that you create needs to be humorous, informative, educational, and engaging. This is the best form of content to create to nurture your prospects in the awareness stage.

- Regardless of the social media sites you use, you must ensure that you are always social. To create a loyal audience, you need to engage and interact with them. This can be done by reposting their posts or even through a simple shoutout to acknowledge the support and love your followers show your business. Always reply to comments and the messages you receive. If you appreciate your audience, they will soon start to reciprocate this sentiment. Another simple means to boost engagement is by asking questions.

- You must not use social media platforms as a means to deliver sales pitches all the time. Instead of telling them about how wonderful your products are, you can work on showing them how the products work, and the different benefits they can gain by using those products. By posting customer testimonials and reviews, you can develop the necessary social proof about your business.

- Start using hashtags specific to your business or any trending hashtags in your niche to create awareness about your business. By using the right hashtags, you can increase the visibility of posts on social media.

- You can work with influencers in your niche to create ads for Facebook or Instagram. By collaborating with influencers, you can organically grow the number of followers on social media profiles. Not just that, it is a great way to market to the influencer's existing followers along with your own followers.

Chapter 5: Second Stop - The Discovery Phase

The second stage of the sales funnel is the discovery phase. At this point, the prospect is quite interested in your business or the product you are selling. Even if they are interested, the prospects aren't ready for a sales pitch or even a conversation with a salesperson, not yet. Your idea is to keep continuing the education process you started in the previous step. You must keep providing them with new and updated information about your products or services. At this stage, the content needs to be informative, educational, and engaging. The best formats for content creation are case studies, demo videos, and webinars.

At this stage, you can start collecting leads and identifying their actions, which can help move them along to the next stage. For instance, if you are hosting webinars to engage your audience at this stage, then your aim needs to be to gently nudge them into moving onto the third stage of the sales funnel. The likelihood of those viewers who attend your webinar converting into your customers is quite high. Remember that the prospects are already interested in your business, but they need more information. Don't try to push them for a hard sell at this point. You merely need to work on nurturing the relationship you establish with them in the previous stage.

A lot of sales professionals tend to think of the discovery stage of the sales cycle as a stage wherein they can learn more about their prospective clients. This is an incredibly important aspect of the discovery phase, but there is so much more to it. As a business owner, you must place yourself in the shoes of your prospective customer and try to understand the customer journey.

You must remember that the prospect's goal at this stage in the sales cycle is recognizing their own needs. The potential buyers tend to ask themselves the following questions in the second phase of the sales funnel.

- Do I really have a need right now?
- How is that affecting my organization on a personal level or me?
- What is not going to be affected if I leave my need unaddressed?

If the buyers are seeking this while interacting with your business, then your objectives as a seller become quite clear. Your primary objective is to help the customer get a better understanding of their needs and the consequences they stand to face if their need is left unaddressed. Therefore, the goal of the discovery phase of the sales funnel can mean the following.

- To identify any critical business issue the prospect faces at this stage.

- Try to surface and intensify the awareness of their need or problem and the consequences of not solving the need or problem.
- Try to help the buyer solve their problem or help satisfy their needs.

If you or your business can help achieve these three steps, then it will help establish and deepen the trust the buyer places in your business. However, how can you successfully identify, intensify, and internalize the discovery stage? The simple answer to this question is by finding the optimum balance between gathering information and sharing insights with the customer. You must not riddle the customer with a lot of questions. This is not the time to grill the prospect about anything. You must merely help the prospect understand the importance of addressing their needs or problem immediately.

Pique Their Interest

You need to work on piquing the interest of your prospects in your business or products so that they stick around. It is rather easy to sell to those who are interested in your products. The prospects might have done the basic research and have concluded that their solution lies with your business. Now, all that you must do is answer some of their questions, make sure that you get in touch with them, and stop them from going over to your competitors. However, how do you ensure that the prospects stay interested in your products? You cannot start a relationship with someone who isn't actively looking for a solution or trying to fulfill a need. This might be rather challenging. However, it is not impossible to accomplish. Here are a couple of simple things you can do to increase the interest of your prospects in your business.

Don't sell the product

Not everybody that you try selling to will be interested in purchasing your products. However, there is one thing that everyone is interested in, and that is their own selves. You must try to create a vision of what is going to happen once they purchase your product. This is a simple yet great way of increasing the interest of your prospects in what you are selling. For instance, think about Nike's caption- "Just Do It," or Burger King's slogan - "Have it your way." These captions and slogans don't tell you what the brand offers, but they do tell you what you can do by using their products. You must keep in mind that the prospect is interested in your business, but it is time to pique their curiosity about what you offer. The harder you try to pitch selling to them, the sooner will they drop out of the sales funnel. Instead, it is about making them curious about what your product can do and how it will help add value to their lives, which will make them stick around. For instance, if you are a copywriting firm, then you can go through the prospect's website, look for any possible errors, and then email the prospect with certain corrections and add the line "as your copywriter, I am happy to say that now your website will be 100% typo-free, always."

The sales and marketing professional who comes across as reliable and trustworthy is the one who is likely to be able to convince prospects of the desirability of buying the product or service promoted by him. Nothing conveys that better than the ability to solve problems.

Say you are a furniture salesman who is trying to sell a dining table to a customer and the only thing that keeps you from convincing him to commit himself is the fact that he prefers the table in a different shade, which your store does not have in stock. If you solve his problem by promising him that you will organize to get it from the head-office warehouse in the next four days, he will seal the deal. What worked for you here is not any fancy sales talk or glib promotion of some other dining table he did not want, but your ability to solve his problem.

Rather than worrying about the fact that you may not be an extrovert, which is merely a personality trait, you should focus on your ability as a problem solver. If you earn the reputation of a salesperson who is also an ace problem solver, both employers and customers will place a premium on your services and prefer to work with you than anyone else.

You can be biased

A lot of salespersons tend to pretend like they are unbiased to sound more credible. However, you must remember that your prospects probably know that you will be biased toward your products and business. In fact, there isn't a thing you can do to convince the customer that your opinions are unbiased. So, it is better to drop the pretense and instead redirect these efforts toward moving them along the sales funnel. It is better that you simply embrace your excitement for your products. If you believe that your products are the best there are in the market, then it is your opinion to which you are entitled. You need to merely share your opinion with your prospects and show your commitment to that opinion. Doing this will make your opinion seem more genuine and natural. This, in turn, will make the prospect believe what you are saying.

Learn from your prospect

Another simple way to increase engagement and keep the prospects interested is by making sure that your prospect feels heard and respected. Everyone likes being heard and acknowledged. If your prospect has any questions, ensure that you answer them as quickly as you can. This is not only a sign of professionalism, but it will make the prospect feel like their queries are valid. If your prospect expresses their opinions, then you must ensure that you acknowledge the same.

Build Lasting Relationships

The focus of a lot of business owners happens to be gathering new customers. However, you cannot let gaining new customers to be your sole focus. If you want to increase your sales, then you need to build good relations with all those prospects who enter the sales funnel. If you don't establish good relations, then the chances of the prospects dropping out of the sales funnel increase.

Now that you have developed the customer personas for your business, it is time to use that information to build good customer relationships. The customer personas will help you understand what the prospects are looking for at different stages of the sales funnel and you can use this knowledge to provide them exactly what they need. In this section, you will learn about the different things you can do to build a relationship and establish trust.

Good communication

You need to ensure that timely and efficient communication is a priority for your business. It doesn't mean that communicating with a single prospect must encroach into your business's productivity. However, if you can demonstrate to the prospects that you are available when they need you, it does show that customer satisfaction is your priority. You must also make it a point to answer the queries your prospects have and address any of their concerns. If you do this in a timely fashion, it shows that you take their concerns seriously.

Tell a story

Customers like interacting with a company they feel is "real." They generally don't want to purchase from or develop a consumer relationship with a corporate drone that they can't identify with. Connect with your customers by showing them that you and all the people who work with you in the company are real people. While most businesses only include their story on their website's About Us page, it's important to keep the idea circulating. You don't have to push that you're down to earth and your company is all about helping people because that can start to feel insincere. Instead, use your marketing campaigns to tell a story.

The point is to let your potential customers feel like they're a part of something bigger. If their presence positively affects your business and they know that, they'll be more likely to stick around. It's a well-known fact that we like to do things that make us feel like we're good people, so make sure your customers know they're a part of your story. You can do this by posting customer testimonials and photos, describing how your product helped someone, or even share a behind the scenes look that reminds your customers that their purchases affect many lives, not just your company's bottom line. When potential customers see this kind of community building, they start to realize that they're not just buying a product - they're buying into a niche group.

Positive attitude

You must ensure that all the communications you have with your prospects are always positive. As a business owner, you must train all your employees who deal with prospects to stay positive at all times. Exuding energy and confidence makes the prospects trust you, and they will also feel like being involved with your business. Enthusiasm and zeal tend to be quite infectious. So, you can attract optimistic responses from your prospects if you stay positive.

Customer service

If you have a specific business channel or dedicated staff who respond to customers, then you must ensure that the channels are fully optimized. You can also switch to online customer assistance to make it easier for your customers to reach you. This is a simple yet brilliant means to add value to the customer journey and will make you stand apart from your competitors. It also helps in generating positive word-of-mouth publicity for your business. Prompt and efficient customer service is important to ensure a good customer journey experience.

Exceed their expectations

Your prospects will certainly have some expectations about the products or services you offer. The idea is to exceed their expectations. You must ensure that you deliver what you promise if you want to establish good customer relationships. A simple tactic used by businesses is to underpromise and overdeliver. When you can exceed the customer's expectations, it will certainly impress them and keep them coming back for more. It can be something as simple as delivering a product sooner than the promised date of delivery. For instance, you can promise to deliver a product within a week, knowing full well that it can be delivered within two days. So, when the delivery does reach the customer earlier than anticipated, it will make them feel like you are working hard to keep your promises.

Online presence

You can use your online social media accounts, blogs, and business website to engage your prospects. Promptly respond to their queries, provide them with useful information, and give them all the details they need about your products. By doing these simple things, you can ensure that your prospects stay interested in your business.

Having an online presence also shows that you can be trusted. By establishing trust with your prospects, you will be able to portray your business as an industry expert. Once the prospects begin to see that you not only talk the talk but can walk the walk too, they will start to think of your business as a trusted source of information.

Build Rapport with All Customers

If you want to build a relationship with a potential customer or customers, you should always investigate before the meeting. If you know something about your potential customer, you can always prepare a few questions or comments that will improve the discussion. For example, if you find that your potential client or customer breeds Golden Retriever puppies, it would be nice to learn more about dogs. This does not mean that you should become an expert. You should find enough information about Golden Retrievers and ask a potential customer some interesting questions. A potential customer would like to share this information with you and look forward to sharing with you something that interests him.

Many people do not use traditional methods to build mutual understanding because they believe that this is fake. You may not be interested in Golden Retrievers or other topics that may interest your potential client, but you need to spend some time listening to someone who talks about them. You do this because you have to make a sale. There is some truth in this objection, but it is important to establish a mutual understanding with the customer before concluding a sale.

People will never buy a product from people they do not trust, but they will almost always buy from someone they like. For the most part, they will buy from someone who looks like them. If you meet someone with similar tastes, you will feel comfortable in the presence of that person because you know what they are like. That's because you like the same things. In the above example, talking to a potential customer about retrievers shows that you have something in common with them. This gives a potential customer the opportunity to tell you about their dogs, and it is more convenient for them to talk to you. When the conversation goes on to the sale, he or she is ready to listen to you with an open heart.

You must be extremely careful if you want to use this kind of method to build understanding. This is because you need to bring a certain aspect of manipulation with you. It's perfectly acceptable to talk to someone about his or her hobbies, whether you're in the office or at a party. But, you should never go beyond the limit of deception. If you do not like the idea of exhibitions, you should never start a conversation and pretend that you agree. Not only is this wrong, but the potential customer will know that you are not as honest as you say. If you know that a potential customer has a hobby that you disapprove of, you should not discuss it at all. He or she may have many other interests that you can talk about, and there will be something that interests you and fits your perspective.

Even in sales situations, always be authentic. Most customers know when you're being dishonest in order to make a sale, and this will ruin any trust or rapport you had started to build.

Be friendly

A person who is cold to another person will receive the same reaction. You should always approach customers with warmth. You need to smile, make eye contact, give them a firm handshake, and engage them in conversation. Have a system in place to ensure your employees are friendly, too. When customers feel that they are liked, appreciated, and they have a good experience with you and your business, they are more likely to turn into lasting customers.

Show real interest

This was mentioned earlier, but it shouldn't be surprising, as people often focus on themselves. This is a feature that will help you with sales, as you need to know more about your potential customers so that you can identify the best course of action. The buyer always wants to be able to communicate what he thinks, including his fears, problems, or wishes. They always want to feel that they are being heard. The more you show them that you listen to them, the more relaxed they become and the more willing they are to share information.

Find a common language

People often prefer people who are like them. This means that you can disclose some common interests that will help you build a better relationship with your prospective client. Maybe you went to the same school or you were born in the same city. You can also talk about your children if you want to. No matter what it is, you should find similarities that allow you to connect and communicate.

A new salesperson is often sensitive when it comes to the time he or she spends with a customer. They always think that they only have one hour or less to make an impression, and they feel they should use this time to convey all their points. They waste no time talking and dive into the commercial area without icebreakers. That is not a very good strategy. There are cases where there is too much talk and the customer wants to get to work, so always read the person you want to talk to and understand how much time you can spend talking.

You need to make sure that you are yourself, but you need to remember that you have to change your approach depending on the person or company you are selling to. You should never change who you are, just your tone or the way you communicate with people in your environment, depending on the culture.

Tools to Use

Once your prospects learn about your business and are interested in what you offer, you have pretty much gotten them hooked. Now, it is time to reel them in and help them move along the sales funnel so that they convert. Here are a couple of tools you can use to prevent any prospects from getting away.

- Once your prospects visit your website, the last thing you need from them is to drop out of the sales funnel completely. So, you need to be able to create a website that will keep your visitors around. A helpful tool you can use to create engaging and informative landing pages in Unbounce. By ensuring that the prospects stick around for longer, the chances of them converting into paying customers to increase.

- Do you ever think about how others use your site? If yes, then you should use CrazyEgg. This tool displays the different points at which most people click on your page. It essentially gives you heatmaps of all the links the customers click on when they visit your business webpage. You can use this data to optimize your webpages to ensure maximum conversions.

- If you are interested in learning about what each visitor does when they visit your site, then you must start using FullStory. This service essentially records the way prospects navigate your website and even shows the recorded data in the form of a video you can view later.

- If you are interested in collecting information from all those who visit your website, then you need HelloBar. This is a simple service that shows up in the form of a sticky bar on your website. The prospects are required to enter their email address in the sticky bars displayed on the screen so that they can be contacted later.

Additional Tips

There are a couple of simple tips you can follow to establish trust with your customers. The best option available at your disposal is to put up customer testimonials and product reviews of your business and products online. A potential customer would have done all the research they need about your products and business. By going through favorable reviews, it will convince them that choosing your business is in their best interest. You can ask your previous customers for their testimonials or reviews and can strategically place them on your business website and social media accounts.

Now that the customer is aware of the different products or services you offer, it is time to try and tip the scales in your favor. Everyone likes offers and discounts. So, it is time to leverage this fondness for discounts to increase your sales. You can offer discounts or offer higher-end products at a reduced price for a limited time. By creating a temporary sense of urgency, you can convince your prospects to move along the sales funnel.

If you have a brick and mortar store, then you must ensure that you place the address for it on your website and your social media profiles. You must ensure that your prospects can easily contact you. You need to provide viable contact information, including a phone number, address, and email address.

As you are engaging your social media accounts, please remember that you are trying to establish a good rapport with your prospects. The best way to do this is by engaging with them and promptly responding to their comments or queries. The longer you take to respond to the prospects, the less will they be interested in doing business with you.

Chapter 6: Stop Three - Evaluation Begins

If you want to create content which will appeal to your prospects, then you must ensure that you have a thorough understanding of the different phases a buyer goes through. In this chapter, you will learn about the third step in the sales funnel, and that's evaluation. In this section, you will learn about ways in which you can attract traffic, create content which is ideal for prospects in the evaluation phase, and certain tips for marketing yourself to enable conversion.

In this stage, your prospects are aware of their problem or need, are interested in the solution or products you offer and are now considering all the options available to them. These prospects are essentially evaluating the solution or products your business offers. Now that we have defined this stage, it is time to start decoding this stage of the customer journey.

So, what are the different thoughts that you might have at this stage? You might be wondering about how you can attract more customers. Or maybe you are thinking about ways in which you can increase the traffic to your site. Do you want to learn about techniques that can help in moving the customer to the final stage of the sales funnel from this stage? Are you wondering about how you can manage your social media accounts? It is normal to have all these thoughts, and you can answer them once you go through the information in this section.

Here are certain questions that you must ask yourself while deciding on the kind of content your prospects will need at this stage.

- What are the different types of solutions the prospects can investigate?
- How will the prospects educate themselves about the different options available?
- How do they analyze the pros and cons of each option?
- How do the buyers decide which solution is good for them?

By answering these questions, you will have the insights you need to create the ideal content along with the keywords you must use for leveraging your content.

What do the buyers usually look for in this stage of the sales funnel? Most of the prospects in this stage tend to compare the different solutions available to solve their problems. As a business owner, it is your duty to help answer their questions and provide them with helpful information, which in turn will encourage their conversion. A majority of buyers tend to search for information at this stage and haven't made up their mind about making a purchase, at least not yet. The world wide web offers a plethora of information to the prospects. When you are thinking about marketing to those in this stage of the sales funnel, you must not only understand what they are seeking, but what they are looking at, too. You must refocus your efforts on the content that your prospects view. A little research and you will be able to determine the kind of content which attracts response from the buyers.

What are the different pages the prospects will visit in this stage? Your prospects will be visiting those pages which include the keywords they are looking for. So, you must make it a point to include such keywords and phrases in the content you create, which will attract your prospect's attention. The different formats of content which will work well in this stage include blog posts, any downloadable content, and email marketing.

Prospects will want to decide based on their logic, even if it is known that you can persuade the buyers with emotion. So, this is your chance to appeal to the logic of your prospects, and you can use quantifiable data for compelling them emotionally to choose the solution you offer. You must be knowledgeable about and explain the best course of action to them and must give them examples or even case studies to show the outcomes they can expect. To do this, you can rely on the positive experiences other customers had in the past, like customer testimonials. You can use your knowledge about the industry as well as the understanding of their issue to offer them a solution.

Compelling, well thought out, and well-written content which addresses the specific needs of the prospects will help them understand the different challenges they are facing and the cost of solving the problem. As you have been trying to establish in the previous steps, you are an industry expert, and you must offer your expertise to your prospects. The information you are providing your prospects must be in sync with the wants and needs of the customer personas you have developed.

You need to earn the prospect's trust. So, you must help further their understanding of their problems. You need to examine your customer and the customer personas carefully. Here are some questions you must ask yourself at this stage.

- What is the customer's purchase behavior?
- What kind of research and information does the prospect need at this stage?
- Are there any essential keywords or relevant phrases that the prospect will use at this stage to facilitate their research?

To write content which is appealing, searchable, and conversion-inducing, you must use your in-depth understanding of the ways the prospects can use your products. The content needs to directly address the concerns as well as the goals of the prospects. Here are a couple of topics you can use to relate to the prospect.

- The prospect's approval process.
- Their specific environment and the different steps they must go through to implement your solution and

optimize the returns.

- The usual challenges or obstacles that will come their way while using the product.

- The different opportunities which will crop up while they are using your solution to satisfy their need or address their issues.

- The different unique experiences a specific customer's persona will experience from the stage of recognizing their needs, understanding their problem, finding the best solution, and making the purchase.

The best format to offer content to the prospects at this stage includes lists of pros and cons, comparisons, expert advice, and even live interaction.

If you have content already, you might be wondering if you can use it by repurposing or refreshing the older content in this stage. Well, you can repurpose old content if you do the following.

- Take stock of all the content available to you.

- You need to delete or edit it such that all the vague verbiage or any ambiguity present in it has been deleted.

- You need to update it with recent facts and data.

- You can use all the existing content and propose the information in the form of an attractive offer.

- You can modify or even create a new landing page for providing your new offer to the prospects.

A landing page is a web page your prospects will end up on after they click your business link. This is one of the best marketing tools you have at your disposal, and when you create effective landing pages, you can encourage your prospects to move onto the next phase of the sales funnel. You must understand that your prospect is willing to exchange some information if you provide them with an irresistible offer. The offer you propose must be such that it brings the prospects a step closer to solving their problem or need.

So, what are the different elements that must be included in the landing page at this stage? The first thing to be included is an attractive title for the offer. You must use certain keywords and phrases that your prospects might be looking for, like "tips to," "how-to," "what to," etc. You must not forget to use specific terms related to the products or services you offer like "fashion," "real estate," "marketing," or the like. You need to include a small paragraph describing all that you are offering your prospects. You need to explain how the prospects will benefit from your offer and how it will add value to their lives if they decide to accept it. You need to include bulleted impact statements which describe the key features you want prospects to focus on while going through the content you provide them. Apart from this, you must include a CTA button and form fields. The CTA button you design must encourage the prospects to take some action which will move them along the sales funnel.

Now that you have created a well-optimized landing page, the next thing you must be wondering about is how you can direct your leads to that page. Well, the answer is simple - you need to create content which will be relevant, helpful, and informative to the prospects.

Are there any specific key terms and phrases you must use in the content that you create for this stage? As mentioned earlier, the sole focus of prospects at this stage is to look for different options that will help them solve their issues. You must try to optimize and maximize your online traffic by including certain keywords and phrases. Here are a couple of examples of how you can design the content for this stage of the sales funnel.

You can include solution-specific terms in the content like "improve," "fix," or "redesign." The landing page will also be a part of the search results the prospects will search for, so it needs to offer them a concrete solution. You must call attention to your industry expertise along with the products or services you offer. Start thinking like your prospects or use your buyer personas to understand the different words and phrases you can incorporate in the content you create. All the key terms you make a note of need to be present in your offer title, the copy of the landing page, the CTA button, emails you send, the email subject line, post titles, and all the posts on social media.

Once you manage to attract your prospects, the next step is to guide and nurture them into the next stage of the sales funnel. Establishing a relationship based on trust with your prospect is quite important at this stage. If they are not prepared to move onto the next stage, then you need to stay in touch with them and slowly nudge them in the desired direction. You can send strategically planned emails to help them along. They might even need a little reassurance along with some hand-holding at this stage. Use the tips mentioned in the previous step to establish trust and your reputation as a problem-solver in the industry. You can send them information about other customer success stories, lists of product comparisons, any company-related news, and provide them all the research which will give them a better understanding of the solution you are proposing.

The continuous stream of interaction will ensure that your business or products are a part of your prospect's thought process. Once you do all this, it is time to pass on the lead to the marketing or the sales team. You must do this to ensure that they move along the sales funnel and close the deal instead of dropping out of sight. How will you determine when a prospect is ready to leap? You must start using sales tactics when you notice that the information being used by the prospect is no longer in the consideration phase, when the prospect starts looking at the pricing plans or pages, or when the prospect requests to talk with a sales rep.

Principles of Persuasion

There are certain principles of persuasion you can use in the evaluation phase of the sales funnel, and they are discussed in this section. Dr. Robert Cialdini described six principles of persuasion, which were explained in his famous book, "Influence." Three of those principles can be employed by you when you are trying to convert your prospects and move them toward the final stage of the sales funnel. For more than sixty years, researchers have been trying to understand the different factors which influence people to say "yes" to others. There is no doubt that persuasion is a subtle art by itself, but there is a surprising amount of science which is involved in this equation. Whenever someone needs to make a decision, it certainly sounds nice to think that they consider all the information available at their disposal, and this determines their thinking process. However, the truth is quite different. We all tend to lead extremely stressful lives. In this busy world that we live in, we constantly seek shortcuts to help guide our decision-making process and reduce the amount of thinking that one needs to undergo. There are six universal shortcuts that dictate human behavior, and they are reciprocity, authority, scarcity, liking, consistency, and consensus. The three principles of persuasion you will learn about in this section are reciprocity, scarcity, and authority. By understanding these principles and using them ethically, you can help in increasing your chances of persuading your prospects to convert into paying customers. Let us learn more about each of these principles.

Reciprocity

The first principle of influence, according to Cialdini, is that of reciprocity. It essentially states that people feel obligated to give back to others the form of service, gift, or even behavior that they have received from them. For instance, did you ever feel like you were obliged to invite someone to a party because they had invited you to a party in the past? If someone does you a favor, you automatically assume that you owe them a favor regardless of whether the same is stated or not. When it comes to social obligations, people are quite likely to say yes to those whom they owe something.

One of the best demos of the principle of reciprocity in action comes from a series of experiments conducted in a restaurant. Think about a situation where you go to a restaurant, and the waiter gives you a gift. Perhaps while bringing the bill to your table, the waiter gives you a free fortune cookie, a piece of cake, or maybe even a mint. So, the question is, will this gift you receive have any influence in determining the tip you leave the waiter? A lot of people might say that it will not have any effect. However, that simple mint which was offered can make a lot of difference. In a study that was conducted while researching the validity of this principle, it was noticed that the tips given by patrons who were given a free mint at the end of their meal increased by about 3%. It is interesting to note that when the patrons were offered two mints, the tips didn't double. The amount given as tips quadrupled, and it resulted in a 14% increase in tips given to the waiter. However, the most interesting thing about this experiment is that in one scenario the waiter walks away after giving a free mint, and then turns back and offers another mint to the patrons along with a compliment. The instances wherein this was done, a whopping 23% increase in tips was noted. It is not merely about trying to influence others that matters; it is also about the way you influence them. So, to use the principle of reciprocity, you must ensure that you are the first one to give something personalized and rather unexpected.

When you are trying to move the prospects along the sales funnel, you can use this simple principle. It is about doing something for someone without establishing a quid pro quo. You can use this principle while creating content. You can provide free access to certain content without asking visitors to register. When you send your prospects content or even give them free advice, it makes the prospects more susceptible to persuasion later.

Scarcity

The second principle of persuasion propounded by Cialdini is scarcity. It essentially states that the demand for those things is always higher when they are scarce. In 2003, British Airways announced that they would not be operating the London to New York Concorde flight twice a day because it became uneconomical for the airlines to maintain. The day after this announcement was made, the sales for this flight service increased drastically. Observe that there was nothing that changed about Concorde itself. The flight time didn't decrease, there was no change in the service, and the airfare didn't decrease. The only difference was that it became a scarce resource. The result of this was that the demand for it increased.

So, when it comes to persuading others to act the way you want them to, the principle of scarcity wins. It is not sufficient to merely tell others the benefits they can gain if they choose the products or services you offer. You must also make it a point to tell them what makes your business unique. Tell your prospects about what they will lose if they don't consider your offer. This tends to create a sense of scarcity, which in turn prompts them to act quickly.

The human psyche is such that the chances of purchase increase if the prospects are informed that a special offer will expire soon or if they are told that it is the last product available. Essentially, people will come to believe that they will miss out on something they must have if they don't act quickly. This is a principle of persuasion that is commonly used by businesses to increase their rate of conversion. For instance, Orbitz.com included a line "Act fast! Only two tickets are left at this price!" in one of their ads. This tells the prospects that the supply of air tickets is limited and will not last long. By creating a sense of scarcity, Orbitz is trying to convince more prospects to convert. Scarcity can also be time-limited. For instance, if you include a blurb that says "this offer ends in two hours" while listing the products online, it creates a sense of time-bound scarcity. By adopting this principle, you will essentially be giving your prospects the nudge that they need to move in the direction you desire without seeming pushy.

Authority

The principle of authority is based on the idea that people tend to follow those who they perceive as being credible and experts. For instance, the ability of physiotherapists to persuade their patients to comply with their recommended exercise regime increases when they display their medical diplomas for others to see. Another everyday example is that people tend to pay a total stranger for the parking meter if the person requesting the payment is dressed in a uniform instead of casual clothes.

The science involved in this principle is quite simple. When you signal to others that you are a credible and knowledgeable authority, then the chances of them being persuaded to increase. Before you influence them to listen to you, you must first establish that you indeed are credible and knowledgeable. Of course, this can also cause certain problems - you cannot go around talking about your brilliance while interacting with your prospects. However, you can certainly make someone else do this for you. It doesn't matter if the person introducing you is connected to you or not. The only thing that matters is the introduction they give you to the prospects.

In a study, a set of real estate agents were able to increase their number of property appraisals and contracts when they arranged for their receptionists who answered customer inquiries first to mention the credentials and expertise of their colleagues. So, all those customers who were interested in letting out their properties were told something along the lines of, "Lettings? Well, let me connect you with XYZ, who has more than fifteen years of experience in dealing with letting out properties in this area." This led to an overall increase in the number of appointments along with signed contracts.

Take a moment and think about it - people tend to have an innate tendency to obey all authority figures. It is an inherent trait of the human mentality. Certain prefixes or job titles like that of a Dr. tend to make such people seem like authority figures and experts.

ShoeDazzle used this principle to increase their sales. It is an internet startup that sells accessories and shoes for women. It was founded in 2009, and Kim Kardashian is its co-founder. She also acts as one of the chief fashion stylists for this venture. Even though this company was founded by Brian Lee and Robert Shapiro, it didn't help increase conversions or attract more buyers. This happened when the company decided to bring Kim Kardashian on board as a co-founder. Regardless of what your personal feelings are about Kim, she is perceived to be a style icon by most of the young shoppers - the target demographic of ShoeDazzle. This helped in increasing the sales recorded by this venture.

Chapter 7: Final Stop - Seal the Deal

Well, the prospect has a need, has done all the necessary research, and has now decided to make the purchase - finally. All the stages which lead up to the conversion event have been completed. The prospect has come a long way, but this doesn't mean that things have come to an end. Marketing at the final stage of the sales funnel is as important as it was at all the other stages. If you don't take the necessary steps, you can still lose out on a customer. Marketing needs to be quite simple and straightforward at this stage. If you have an online website for sales, then ensure that you carefully test it to make sure that navigating it is easy and not complicated. Are there too many steps involved in this process? Does it take too long to process the requests? Is the website optimized for desktops as well as mobile devices? Ask all these important questions, and the answers to these questions will help determine whether the website is effective and efficient or not. If the purchase process seems too difficult or intimidating to the customer, then you can essentially lose out on a potential customer.

Once the prospect is certain of the solution which works best for them, the prospect enters the decision stage. In this stage, the prospect will be essentially compiling a list of all the different businesses and brands which offer the same solution as yours does. The prospects will them evaluate which option works out the best for them and go with it. Once the prospect has decided upon the product to choose, they enter the final stage of their customer journey. These individuals are no longer your prospective buyers; they are your customers now. They are in a stage where they need to decide whether they are delighted with their decision or not. They are looking forward to gaining all the benefits that the products offer. You must use good customer service at this stage to ensure lasting customer relationships.

Also, you must remember that just because the customer has made a purchase, this doesn't mean the process has ended yet. There is a post-purchase stage wherein you need to work on creating a loyal audience of brand advocates for your business. This stage matters because customer loyalty and advocacy help generate revenue for the business. After a purchase is made, it is an important part wherein the customer needs to decide whether they are happy with the purchase that they made or not. It is time for them to evaluate their decision.

If the customers feel like they made the wrong decision or took the wrong call, then they can easily return their purchase. You can mitigate this risk by ensuring that the customer's journey was a happy one and that they had a pleasant experience dealing with your brand. However, even if you have a satisfied customer, you must understand that the chances of repeat purchases in the future are still not guaranteed. So, to ensure that the customers stay loyal to your business and return in the future for more purchases, you can send them follow-up emails and surveys to understand whether they were satisfied with their experience or not.

The final stages of the sales funnel include evaluation and purchase. In the evaluation phase, the buyers are trying to make up their minds about whether to purchase something or not. Usually, the marketing and the sales teams both need to work closely to convince the prospect that their brand is the best solution for the buyer. Once this is done, the prospect will move onto the purchase stage. This is a chance for the business to leave a positive and lasting impression on the buyer.

Customer Experience Funnel

Here are the different stages of a customer experience funnel that your customers go through.

Repeat

Once the customer makes a purchase, the next thing you need to start concentrating on is to ensure that you transform them into a repeat customer. It means you need to work on customer retention and nurture the customer relations you create along the way. Repeat customers to ensure that you can generate revenue from the existing customer. You will need to work on marketing even after the purchase phase to ensure that the customers keep coming back for more.

Loyalty

In this stage, the customer develops a conscious liking for your business and starts to identify themselves with your brand and business. At this stage, engagement is quite important, and as a business owner, you need to work on nurturing the positive relations and connections you make with the customers.

Referral

Once you have managed to establish the loyalty of the customer for your business, the chances of them referring your business and products to others tend to increase.

Advocacy

You need to concentrate on transforming your loyal customers into advocates of your brand and business. This is the ultimate goal of a business owner for nurturing their existing customers. When your customers are happy with your products and business, they will want to share their positive experiences with others, too. By posting on social media about their positive experience and through word-of-mouth publicity, they tend to become self-appointed advocates of your brand. The publicity and marketing which comes organically from your existing customers is something that cannot be simulated by any other means.

The goal of all these steps is to increase your bottom line by increasing your sales and awareness.

What thoughts does the customer experience at this stage while evaluating the products and your business? The prospect will usually be thinking about the costs involved, the timeline for delivery, the results which are promised by you, and about the customer support they will need along the way. All of the prospects in this stage are trying to understand all the different aspects of their chosen solution fully. The prospects are trying to think about their future once they have their chosen solution ready. This is where content creation steps in. The aim is to understand what your prospects are looking for at this stage and making sure that you can create such content which proves to be relevant to them.

So, what are all the prospects looking for in this stage? In this stage, the prospects are certain that they want to purchase a product from you or pay for the solution you are offering. The prospects have compared the products you offer with those offered by your competitor and are now happy with their choice. However, for them to arrive here, they will need some content and information. As a business owner leading your prospects through the final stage of the sales funnel, it is time to deliver your sales pitch. You need to highlight to the customer the different reasons why they need to opt for your products. You need to explain how your business differs from your competitors and how you are better. Explain the reasons why they need to opt for your solution and explain all the value they stand to gain. While doing all this, you must also make it a point to include information to certain questions the customers might have. The customers might be wondering about how long it will take for your solution to solve their issues and create value as promised. The customers will be thinking about the costs involved and the results you promised.

At this stage, the prospects will be looking for information which will help them make the final call. The information they will be looking for at this stage is about whether the solution you are offering is the best one or not, about how competitive your prices are, and the quality of the products you offer. The two important web pages all the customers will refer to in this stage are the About Us page and the Products and Service page of your business.

The buyers will be paying close attention to your business's About Us page at this stage, and you must design this section such that it creates a professional first impression on the visitors. You must include information about the different services and products that you offer, your business objectives, and goals. You must understand that your buyers are looking for information which will give them the confirmation that your business is indeed the best option available for them. You can also include customer testimonials in this section. By providing case studies along with quantifiable facts, your business will look more trustworthy to potential customers.

The other page that your buyers will be keenly going through is the product and service description pages on your website. The buyers will want to know everything about the products and services you offer before sealing the deal and purchasing something. Keep in mind that the prospects in this stage are looking for certain reassurance to ensure that they are indeed making the right decision. They will carefully go through different pages like the one which displays information about your customer service team, the delivery policies, and the terms and conditions applicable to purchase.

The best forms of offers at this stage which can be made to your potential customers include free trials, live demos, consultations, and any discounted services, product discounts, or coupons.

Principles of Persuasion

Apart from the three principles of persuasion which were discussed in the previous chapter, there are three more that you must focus on. The other principles of persuasion enumerated in Robert Cialdini's book *Influence* are as follows.

Consistency

It is a basic human desire that people like to be consistent with the things they might have said or done in the past.

Consistency is usually triggered by asking and seeking small forms of initial commitments that can be made. In a famous study, researchers noticed that very few individuals were willing to put up an unsightly wooden signboard on their front lawns to support the Drive Safely campaign started in their neighborhoods. However, in a similar neighborhood, about four times as many homeowners indicated that they would be happy to erect a similar signboard. Why is this? Well, ten days before this, all those homeowners had agreed to place a postcard on their front windows which signaled their support for the Drive Safely initiative. The small postcard they were required to put up acted as the small commitment, which led to the bigger change.

So, while trying to influence others, use the consistency principle propounded by Cialdini. The directive of this principle is to seek voluntary, public, and active commitments from others before getting them to do anything.

This principle states that humans have a deep-seated need to be seen as being consistent. As such, once someone has made a public commitment to do something, then the chances of them following through with their commitment increase tremendously. This is based on the psychological makeup of humans, which compels us to act according to the commitments we make. Most marketers use this principle for increasing their rates of conversion. Marketers employ this technique to increase their site visitors by offering them something free of costs like a sample or a guide. Copyblogger, a popular website, uses this principle of persuasion. Copyblogger is a popular blog, but it is essentially a training and software organization that sells content marketing software and tools via Copyblogger Media. On their homepage, you will notice a huge headline urging you to subscribe to the company's free course on online marketing. You merely need to enter your email ID to sign up. This process is seen as a form of public commitment the visitor to the site makes and will make the visitor view themselves as a customer of the company. By doing this, Copyblogger is essentially increasing the chances of its visitors purchasing the services they offer.

Liking

We all tend to prefer to agree with or say yes to those we like. However, what makes one person like someone else? The science of persuasion suggests that there are three important factors at play here. We like those who are similar to us, pay us compliments and cooperate with us. Since most of the interactions take place online these days, it is a good idea to think about how your business can use all these factors in online negotiations. In a series of studies based on negotiations performed between MBA students belonging to two famous B-schools, one group was told that "Time is money. It is time to get down to business immediately." This group recorded a 55% rate of agreement. The other group was told, "Before you can start negotiating, take some time and get to know one another. Identify all the similarities you share and then start the negotiation process." This group managed to have a 90% rate of agreement.

If you want to use the principle of liking, then you need to look for certain similarities you share with others before you can start conducting business. When you like someone, the chances of being influenced by them increase. It is based on sharing certain similar traits or qualities with others you like, and it can be based on something totally superficial like looks. You can increase your rates of conversion by concentrating on the About Us page of your business. Does this idea sound absurd to you? Before you write it off, here is a case study that will make you change your opinion.

A company known as PetRelocation.com assists pet owners globally by helping them relocate with their pets from one country to another. The "About Us" page of this company contains bios of all its staff, and each of the bios included not only show the staff's love for pets, but it also humanizes the qualities of the managers and employees by adding personal details like their hobbies. All of this helps humanize the entire company and increase its likeability, which in turn helps increase its rate of conversion.

Consensus

Especially in times of uncertainty, people tend to look at the actions or behaviors of others to determine their own behavior or action. You might have noticed that several hotels often place a tiny postcard or note in the bathrooms which try to persuade the guests to reuse their linens. Most tend to do this by directing the guest's attention to the different benefits reuse can have on protecting the environment. According to research, it shows that about 35% of guests would comply with such a request. However, is there any means of making this more effective? Well, it was noticed that around 75% of guests who checked into a hotel for over four nights or more tend to reuse their linens at some point during their stay. So, what will happen if you simply use the principle of consensus and place the information stating 75% of guests choose to reuse their linens during the stay and you must, too? Well, by doing this, it was noticed that over 25% of guests complied with this request of reusing linens.

Develop Customer Loyalty and Advocacy

The first thing you need to do is ensure that there is positivity. Positivity is quintessential for inspiring, persuading, and motivating the customers to stay loyal to the business. By opting for a positive approach while marketing, you can ensure that you win your customers over. For instance, by creating an engaging customer experience and providing good customer service, you can elicit positive emotions in your customers. Also, when you promote positivity, it helps improve your sales track record and helps develop customer loyalty. When you make the prospects feel good, they will automatically start to associate your business with positivity and will keep coming back for more.

You must ensure that the customer journey is not about you or your business and is instead all about the customer. When you are trying to influence the customer's thinking, you must shift your attention to the benefits your products can offer them and the way they can add value to their lives. While interacting with the customers, you must ensure that you use the words "you" and "your" instead of self-centric language like "me" or "I." The words "you" and "your" tend to be more persuasive since they directly refer to the listener.

There is always a stage in the sales process wherein a decision needs to be made. Depending on different factors, your prospect will either want to purchase something, or they will drop out of the sales funnel. You can use testers while trying to hold onto any uncertain customers. By giving out testers or free samples, you get a chance to connect with the customer and maybe even convert them into loyal customers of the business.

By establishing brand loyalty, you can easily secure future business. However, before you can reap the benefits it offers, the first step is to create brand loyalty. You can reward your customers with attractive offers or even discounts to motivate them to repeat their purchase. At this stage, you must use your business's message to relate to the customer. By doing this, you can establish loyalty and even form a helpful bond with the customers.

As a business owner, it is quintessential that you understand the importance of having a consistent voice. You must determine your target audience and then get started with marketing. You don't have to try all the different strategies for all your customers. There are some sales and marketing tactics that will work well for certain customers while something else might work for others. Regardless of the tactics you employ, you must ensure that your business can deliver a clear and consistent message across all the different customer touchpoints. If you know what you are offering, it becomes easier to persuade others to get on board.

The customer's awareness of your business along with the relationship they share with your brand are two important factors that influence their decisions. You must work on improving your brand image so that it reflects the values and objectives of your business. Not just that, a good brand image also helps in engaging your customers. Often customers tend to select brands the way they select their friends. They tend to look for certain traits that attract them. Your customers will decide according to the way you make them feel.

You must ensure that you always keep your customers informed about your business. Along with all your products and service offerings, you must also inform them about the different ways in which your products and services can help them. Make it a point to draft newsletters or even greeting cards that you can mail or email your customers at regular intervals. You must ensure that your business website consists of all the information that the customers will need to understand their problems and the ways to fix them.

Something as simple as a handwritten note showing your appreciation can go a long way when you are trying to establish customer loyalty. Your customers will certainly appreciate the fact that you took time out of your schedule to craft handwritten notes for them and have made an effort to get in touch with them. Often the simplest of gestures is all that's required for establishing brand loyalty.

You must ensure that you check in on your customers regularly. If you notice that it has been a while since a customer has made a purchase, you can get your sales team to contact them and find out why. When you make the customers feel valued and important, their chances of turning into loyal advocates of your business tend to increase. A simple phone call can make the customers feel like they are valued members of your business.

Whenever you deal with a customer, make it a point to collect some general information about them like their date of birth, any anniversaries, or dates of other happy occasions. Once you create a database of information about your customers and their information, ensure that you send personalized cards, e-mails, or messages to them on their special occasions. You can set reminders to help you remember all this. Doing this also opens up the door for follow-ups.

If you ever come across any content that you know your customers will value, even if your business does not compose it, make it a point to pass it along to them. By providing them with helpful and useful information, you show the customers that your business only has their best interests in mind.

Chapter 8: Time to Evaluate and Improve

Content Calendar

A content calendar is precisely what it sounds like - it is a calendar detailing the content you wish to publish. Creating a content calendar can help ensure that you are posting the right content at the right time and for the right audience. For instance, say you run a donut store, and one fine day a customer comes in and asks you about your plans for National Donut Day. Well, let us assume that you forgot all about it and this question caught you off guard. If you have a content calendar in place, then the chances of this happening will be quite low since it will give you a precise idea of the content that you must be posting. Here are all the steps you must follow to create a content calendar for your business.

The first thing you need to do is start taking stock of all the current social media marketing efforts you are making. You essentially need to perform a social media audit. The questions you must answer at this stage are as follows.

- What are the different social media platforms you are using?
- Which of these platforms is doing the best marketing

work for you?

- Do you want to keep publishing on all these sites, or do you want to make any changes?
- Is there a possibility of limiting the social media platforms you are using?
- Are there any imposter accounts on these sites you must shut down?
- Do you have a list of all the passwords and usernames for each of your social media accounts?
- How often do you post on each of these accounts?
- Do you have any specific goals for every platform?
- Who maintains these channels for you?

You need to make a note of all this information that will be included in your social media calendar, especially if you are working in a team.

Once you do this, the next step is to perform a content audit. What sort of content do you usually post? Is there any content that seems to be outdated? If yes, then is there any scope to improve that content? Do you need to get rid of any content, or can you develop upon existing content? Also, what type of content usually performs well with your target audience? What sort of content do your competitors post? By answering these simple questions, you will have an idea of the kind of content you can work with and the content that needs to be scrapped.

Now, it is time to familiarize yourself with the network

demographics. Every social media network tends to cater to a specific demographic and a specific audience. The kind of audience present on the network will help guide the type of content you need to create. Most people tend to have accounts on multiple social media channels these days. So, it is quite likely that your customers also follow you on multiple channels. For instance, the audience who follow you on Facebook or Instagram might be older when compared to the audience you have on Snapchat. So, you must make it a point to post content according to the demographics of the audience on a specific network. Understanding your audience is important for the success of a marketing strategy. The good news is that you can easily attain the demographic information of your target audience on any of the major networking sites like Facebook, Instagram, LinkedIn, Twitter, or Snapchat easily. Before you can start devising your content calendar, you must ensure that you understand your audience on those networks.

After you understand your audience, you need to determine the optimum frequency for posting on each of these platforms. Since you have already done your social media audit for your business, you will be aware of your frequency of posting on the existing social media accounts. Will you stick to the same frequency in the future, or do you need to make any changes? Either way, your frequency of posting will help in shaping up your social media content calendar. You need to decide the number of slots you will need per social network. So, the best time to make this decision is right now. You can always tweak it later according to how well your marketing strategies are performing.

The next step is to understand your content ratio. The social media content calendar you create for your business must have some system to categorize the content you want to post. Doing this will help you keep track of the kind of content that your audience seems to like. A common suggestion is to label the content that you create as self-promotional, user-generated and curated content categories. You can also distinguish the content you create according to its formats such as blog posts, announcements, or even videos. The way you want to label the content is entirely your decision. However, regardless of what you decide, you must ensure that the labels you are using are descriptive. It might seem like a time-consuming process at the moment, but it will help save time in the long run. Once you decide on the categories, the next step is to determine the amount of content you want to post in each category.

After this, it is time to establish a content repository. A content repository is a place wherein you can store all the content you want to use while planning your content calendar. Your content repository can be a simple spreadsheet or even an elaborate database. While creating the content repository, there are certain things each piece of content must include, and they are the title, the type of content, relevant links, its expiration date, and any related images or videos. You can also leave some space for any interesting excerpts from content which you can include in your final copy.

The next step is to identify your calendar needs. How detailed must the content calendar be? Do you need to create a separate database or spreadsheet for every type of network you use, or can it all fit in one? Do you need the assistance of your team members to help with this? Who gets to approve the content you want to post? It would be prudent to make the content calendar as detailed as you possibly can, at least during the initial stages. It is better to have more content to choose from instead of having to scramble at the last minute to find good content.

Now that you have gathered all the content you want, it is time to establish a process for posting the content. You need to be quite diligent about setting up a process since it will have a direct effect on the effectiveness of your marketing strategies. You must decide who will be responsible for updating the content calendar. After this, you get to decide who will be responsible for publishing and scheduling all the posts. Figure out if you will need any professional help for developing content. Also, decide where you will be sourcing the images from and if any approval is needed before you can start posting the content. The one final thing you need to determine is how you plan on scheduling the content. Apart from this, you must also make provisions for developing new content. These are certain basic questions you must have answers to before you can place any content in the content calendar. By going through all these steps, you can ensure that your content calendar is properly organized. When it is properly organized, then the chances of any mistakes happening also reduce drastically.

Now you have come to the final step of creating the content calendar, and that is scheduling the time for publishing the content. You have successfully made it through all the steps explained in this section, and now it is time to schedule the publishing time. You can use tools like Hootsuite for scheduling the time for publishing the content.

By creating a content calendar, you can easily automate the process of managing the content on your social media. It might take some time and effort to set it up initially, but once everything is on track, it will help reduce your efforts in the long run.

Measuring Social Media Success

The one thing which makes social media channels quite exciting to use also makes them tricky to measure. Social media platforms tend to undergo constant changes - they keep introducing new features, updating their policies, and making changes to the basic algorithm. All this means that a strategy that might have worked a couple of weeks ago might not make any sense right now. This is the main reason why it is incredibly important to measure the performance of your business on social media. By measuring your social media performance, you can determine whether you have allocated a sufficient social media marketing budget and whether you are using the right tactics or not.

The second problem which comes up is related to measuring the metrics on social media. The metrics are easy to measure, but they don't give you the correct projection of the return on investment. The important metrics like engagement rate, voice share, or even social media reach are tricky to calculate, and you will need online tools to help you calculate these metrics. To measure the success and performance of your social media campaigns, you must follow four steps, and they are given here.

The first step is to set your goals. Before you can start working on developing a marketing campaign, you must determine your goals for the same. What do you plan on achieving with the help of the marketing campaign? Do you wish to increase the traffic to your website or do you want to increase brand awareness? Do you want to reach a larger audience, or do you want to retarget your existing audience? There are various metrics you must use to assess all the results you obtain from the marketing campaign. Before you can measure the results, you must first set certain achievable goals for your business. An achievable goal for your business can be to increase the rate of engagement on Twitter by 20% in the upcoming quarter. That's a good goal because it is a SMART goal. SMART is the acronym you must use for setting goals. The goals you set need to be specific, measurable, actionable, relevant, and they need to be time-bound. So, to set a SMART goal for marketing, you must first determine the specific platform you want to work on. The next step is to ensure that the goal you set can be clearly defined using a metric that can be tracked. The goal must not be unrealistic and needs to be attainable. The goal must also be relevant to your business, and it must be attained within a specific time.

Once you do this, the next step is to select certain metrics to track. After this step, you need to measure the way these metrics are performing monthly. If the metrics seem favorable, then it means your campaign is going along smoothly. If they aren't performing as intended, then it is time to review the campaign and make necessary changes.

Social Media Fails to Avoid

Most marketers believe a marketing campaign cannot be successful without the use of all available channels of social networks. It may not be wrong, but it is not necessary. The social networking platforms you choose should be designed to fit your audience. It makes no sense to develop a brilliant marketing strategy for the platform if your target audience is not even active. Also, the various social networking platforms you use depends on your audience, budget, and campaign. If you have time and budget constraints, focus on one or two platforms instead of all platforms. If you try to use more than two platforms at the same time, it's likely that the content you created will not be personalized for each platform. It's simple: If your audience is not using Twitter, you do not need a Twitter campaign. You do not have to spend your time, energy, and money to develop a campaign that does not generate interest. Use only platforms that are commonly used by your customers and subscribers.

Social networks are not limited to Facebook, LinkedIn, or Twitter. Facebook, Instagram, Twitter, and LinkedIn are popular social networking sites, but they only make up part of the social networking ecosystem. Web forums, email lists, user groups, various photo and video sharing services, podcasts, social bookmark sites, and online niche communities are all part of social networking. You need to remember that you need to make an effort to understand which platforms your customers are using for communication and start getting involved.

Social media is one of the most important marketing methods these days. This does not mean that it is the only marketing tool. There are several aspects of your business that you need to consider. For example, consider SEO, powerful marketing, and branding if you want to develop a comprehensive marketing strategy. For your campaign to succeed, you need to combine different elements. All elements of your campaign should be in complete harmony with each other. Social networks are just one element of your campaign, and you need all the other elements to work together. Traditional marketing methods should be used together with new ones. Instead of relying solely on social networks, you should consider all other aspects.

Some things never change. Yes, there was a complete paradigm shift in the way marketing practices have changed. However, the good old and basic rules of communication, PR, and marketing remain in place. These basics will never go out of style. Knowing the people you influence, the value your business has for their lives, and the ability to develop products and services that help meet their needs are paramount to any good marketing strategy. So, do not deviate from these values if you're considering the possibility of socializing.

Create Sales Funnel on Instagram or Facebook

Without the right marketing strategy, your business will eventually fail due to a lack of customers. Nobody will know about your business, what you offer, and where exactly your products are available. So, if you have not invested time and effort in this mission, now is the time. The easiest way to start is to use a sales funnel, which has been described in detail.

Put simply; the sales funnel shows the perfect way in which a potential customer becomes a customer. Even if you can sell your products or services to thousands of people, few will provide contact information and become leaders. Only a small proportion of these potential customers become customers.

Instagram advertising has proven to be incredibly useful to businesses and organizations of all types and sizes when it comes to marketing. Currently, Instagram Advertising is managed through the Facebook Ads Manager control panel. This makes it easy to sync with your paid efforts on Facebook and allows you to use a variety of targeting options. If you get it in an appropriate area where you can make a profit with every transaction, you can scale the campaign, increase your budget, and achieve greater success.

Start with your Profile Bio. This is your main property without much space to place what you want. You need to use the space by publishing only what your audience finds useful and what will draw them closer to yourself and your brand. If you're selling Instagram funnels, you'll need to use this section to create a compelling call to action. The application does not have much room for text or links throughout the user interface. That's why you need to be creative and use what you have to the best of your ability.

E-commerce products work especially well when managed by user-generated content. This includes using other customers to advertise to potential customers for your products. This can help you put an Instagram sales funnel into practice. So, persuade subscribers to post photos of the product you're using, add tags to your account, or use your corporate hashtag. If you have powerful people, you will kill it!

Custom content develops a culture around your brand, creates a true consumer, and helps raise awareness. With this tactic, you can build an online community that focuses on your business. This means that you have full customer support and benevolence. Resubmitting photos created by users will prompt your audience to participate and buy if they do not have a product. Ultimately, you need to develop constant interaction, increase brand awareness, and turn most of your subscribers into customers.

With the right strategy, your brand can count on a strategic partnership with a well-known, influential person. Make sure you get a high return on your investment in terms of conversion and brand awareness and evaluate it carefully. Working with influential people, you can leverage their network and brand to raise awareness of your e-commerce offerings. They will benefit from their success and popularity.

This method of disseminating your marketing message is not considered advertising because the message comes from the personal and real voice of an influential person. Followers continue to welcome the approval of trusted Instagram stars and influential people, even with stricter restrictions on the transparency of sponsored content.

Chapter 9: Additional Ideas for Automation

You can understand how important it is to start marketing or promoting your business. However, it is possible that part of you will continue to tell you that you can start after a while. This is basic human nature. We tend to postpone unpleasant things for a while. Marketing is not unpleasant by any means, but if you're trying it for the first time, you'll probably feel a little overwhelmed. The deferral begins, and the work is not completed. This can happen several times, and even if your intentions are good, the delay in getting to work can affect your bottom line. You can pause for a while, and at the end of the day, you have no energy left for the task. This behavior should be avoided. You cannot keep it on the back burner and you need to get cracking as soon as you can. You must have the right system that supports you. Do not say, "I'll do it later." This "later" will never come. Get started with your marketing tactics as soon as you possibly can. If you do not want to do daily marketing, you can schedule one day for it. On the agreed day, you should pay particular attention to promotions and nothing else. This avoids unnecessary distractions, and a timeline is always helpful. You will not feel overwhelmed, and you will know that you have enough time to get things done. There are several ways to automate this process. Here are some tools to help you with this process:

- There are several tools like GetDrip and other autoresponders that let you download a bunch of emails that need to be sent in a specific order to set up a simple drip campaign. You can easily add people to the list and then let the automator take over.

- There are several social media management tools such as Buffer, Hootsuite, and many others that allow you to pre-author all your posts on social networks and then strategically place them on multiple media platforms.

- You should also start planning your blog entries. Using various content management systems, such as WordPress, allows you to create multiple blog posts at once and set up their publishing at a specific time in the future.

Social Media Tools

There are different social media tools you can use, and the options available these days can be rather overwhelming. In this section, you will learn about the best social media tools you can use for improving your marketing efforts.

Mention

This tool is quite similar to Google alerts, but it is meant for social media. As the name suggests, this tool will help you monitor your online presence effectively. It also has certain features that allow you to respond to any mention of your business or brand name online. It also allows you to share any news you might have come across about your business in the industry.

Buffer

It is an analytical tool that includes social media publishing in it. It is quite a helpful social media tool that helps send your updates across various social networking sites like Facebook, Twitter, Google+, and LinkedIn. It comes with a prebuilt analytical system that not only helps you check why certain posts of yours seem to be doing better than others but also helps you understand the optimal time for posting content online. The features offered by Buffer also allow you to work along with your team for optimally maintaining your social media profiles.

Feedly

Feedly is a tool that helps with content discovery and helps you find helpful and useful content. It not only allows you to find good quality content, but it also enables you to share the content that you find with your target audience easily. You have the option to subscribe to the RSS feed so that you can stay updated about all the different updates in the industry that are being posted online. If you are interested in a specific topic, then you can use Feedly to track content that is similar to the kind of content that you like.

Twitter Counter

Well, the name of this tool is pretty self-explanatory. This is an online tool that will help you track all the changes associated with your followers, and it also enables you to make predictions and assumptions related to the growth of your followers over a certain period. After a point, it can become rather cumbersome to keep track of the way your Twitter account grows. This free tool comes in handy at such times. It will enable you to understand the growth rate of your followers. You can use these numbers to analyze whether the content you are posting is helping you attain new followers or not.

Bottlenose

This comes with an inbuilt search engine that can be used in real-time, and it helps in consolidating all your marketing efforts on different social media sites along with any other groups. The resultant data is displayed in the order of algorithmic importance. When you have all the information that you need in a logical manner, it becomes easier to analyze and share the results thus obtained. Another feature is that this tool can be integrated with Buffer. So, you can use a combination of these tools for scheduling your social media posts.

Paid Advertising

Paid advertising will help you reach out to your customers rather easily. According to a study that was conducted in 2014, over 80% of online customers tend to research before they purchase anything, and a majority of these customers start their search with a search engine. The best idea to advertise is to advertise on those platforms they use. Newspaper ads have become rather obsolete these days. In this age of digital marketing, the simplest means to start advertising about your business is to start using Pay Per Click or PPC ads like the ones that you will notice in Google's network. This option allows you to present your business as an answer to the customer's queries searched for in the search engine. If, for example, you try to search for "St. Louis, video agency" in Google, then you will notice The Storyteller Studios as one of the top results.

Although many businesses advertise on Google to reach a large global audience, you can also advertise on other networks. If you are aware of your target audience, then you can start using Facebook ads to promote your business on Facebook. However, before you do this, there is one thing you must do - you need to check for the platforms your target audience uses regularly. Once you have a list of all the platforms, you can use paid forms of advertisements on those platforms.

Paid advertising will help in increasing the credibility and awareness of your business. In the long run, a good quality product or quality service will strengthen the reputation of your business. In the short term, there is a component that improves the perception of your business in the eyes of potential customers, and that's advertising. In the short run, a fake it until you make it approach is often assumed by advertisers. When others can see an ad for your business (particularly good advertising), they automatically seem to assume that a business has money. If they think that a business has sufficient funds, then they also think that the business is doing well, which in turn implies that the business has customers. All these things help in establishing your social proof.

Paid advertising gives you the option to target your ads well. Different platforms like Google or Facebook tend to have access to vast amounts of data. It means that these platforms are capable of placing your ads in front of your desired audience. Google will not show you results for doctors in your area if you are searching for saloons online. Also, Facebook's algorithm is designed such that it will not show an insurance advertisement to an 18-year old student's profile. These platforms not only have the necessary data for proper placement of your ads, but they also have the incentive to help with proper placement of your ads. You will want other users to click on your ads, and since you will be paying for every click you receive, the ads will be placed strategically to increase the number of clicks you get. Also, they want those individuals who click ads to be the ones who are most likely to make a purchase. You will continue to advertise only if you see a return on your investment. You can easily obtain demographic data about your target audience online and then use the same for creating paid-for advertisement campaigns.

Paid advertising also allows you to access helpful analytical and monitoring tools. Google AdWords and Facebook Ads Manager measure the results and check how each campaign works. You can also easily view any demographic information that you need about the type of audience that is viewing your ads. You can then use this data to create well-targeted ad campaigns in the future. You can also see the devices that people use most often when interacting with your ad, make a note of the time when the ads get the most engagement, and even set up your profile such that it shows you only those metrics you want to collect.

As a small business owner, you might not have sufficient time to keep monitoring or reporting on your marketing campaign. Hiring a social media manager is an expensive move. You don't have to worry anymore about these things if you start using paid advertising options.

Perfect Your Sales Pitch

It's never easy to create the perfect sales pitch. This is because you need to identify your target customers and spend some time collecting customer information. Then you should invest enough time to analyze your customer information. It can be both expensive and time-consuming, the amount of time and money you spend changing the plan that benefits your business. If you are looking for your audience, follow these steps.

If you do not have a specific customer, it's difficult for you to get in touch with your potential customers. Therefore, you should consult your current customers and also look at the members of your target group. Then, you can figure out how to present a product or service to that audience and identify what's missing in the product or service you're currently offering. Then you should appeal to a broad audience to identify those customers who may be interested in your product or service. You should then use the collected data to design the brand or product to match the target audience. If you know who the audience is, you can write down your sales pitch and increase sales with this step.

When deciding what type of business value or strategy to use in the industry, you should watch what your competitors are doing. This is a cost-effective strategy that will give you some ideas for your commercial offer. You also have the opportunity to identify gaps in your competitor's approach. Then you can use your research to create a reliable sales strategy. When you enter a business, follow the audience of your competitors so you can use them as an example and improve your products and services to serve the customers better.

You should always make sure that you are present on social networks. You have to make a little more effort to keep your customers. This means that you need to make additional efforts on Twitter, Facebook, and Instagram to influence your target audience. Many companies use their accounts to promote their products and services. If you are a smart seller, you can always post some interesting articles or give interesting answers. This shows people that the person working with the site is not indifferent. Some companies are always helping their clients find new ways to use their products or services. They also help them to solve any problems.

Paul English, when he was the head of Kayak, always put a phone in the middle of the room. This phone was used to receive complaints from customers and had a loud and annoying tone. This phone guaranteed that everyone, including English, answered every complaint. Zappo's Tony Xie valued customer service and made sure every new employee was trained to serve customers no matter what they did. There was a time when they had to go to a competing store to buy the shoes the buyer wanted. The essence of these examples is that you should always look after your customers and potential customers and solve their problems as quickly as possible.

Affiliate marketing has been around since the origins of the Internet. Most people do not notice this, but this is a great way to increase your brand awareness. There are many affiliate networks through which you can promote your product. These networks use Pay Per Click or Pay Per Action methods to evaluate potential customers. Amazon, eBay, and some other marketing companies have their partner network, but you can always use other networks if you want.

When it comes to sales or marketing, the only task that takes most of the time is building potential customers. This includes analyzing customer data, their hobbies, professional activities, and social media activities, conducting online and offline surveys, and updating user data annually. Many companies are now in the market to help you do the same. One of the best ways to attract potential customers is to send them personalized emails or newsletters. You can also send them personalized products or services. You must use the data collected to optimize all your efforts and develop a better sales strategy. This may require a lot of work, but you can use companies like Lead Genius to develop and attract new prospects without wasting time.

Many new companies are joining markets that are overburdening the industry. Therefore, it is very difficult to highlight and collect the target group. If you want to create an audience, you need to make sure that you are trustworthy. Over 88% of consumers use online reviews before making a purchase. So, contact the people who wrote multiple reviews and send them something to write a review on. As your business grows in size, you should first place some internal content on the site. Always use your name if you want to gain trust, as this will allow the target audience to connect with the person rather than the company or product.

It's always helpful to interact with all the key players in your industry. This increases the target audience. If you can attract the attention of an influential person or an influential leader, you can also captivate their followers. This will help you build trust and confidence. You need to contact the right entrepreneurs and bloggers at conferences or in social networks. Send them interesting information that is relevant to you, your company, and the product you are selling.

You should always try to post relevant information on your company's website or blog so that your customers know your business well enough. You can always post information about where the company is and how it is developing. The content that you publish does not have to be self-promotion, but you should always talk about the meaning of the product you are offering or the service you offer. You can also talk about ways to solve industry issues or issues your audience faces every day. Try to share wisdom and inspire people who share your interests. If you do not have many people who can write, you can ask some online companies or platforms for help.

Mistakes to Avoid

There are certain mistakes you must avoid if you want to create a good sales funnel which will help improve your conversions. In this section, you will learn about the common mistakes you must avoid increasing the efficiency of your marketing efforts.

A common mistake that a lot of marketers make is that they don't track sufficient data. Most marketers tend to concentrate only on their major metrics like the number of views per page, the conversion rate of visitors, or even the bounce rates. They do this at the risk of ignoring other smaller but equally important metrics like return visitors, scroll patterns, or even the exit pages. This is one mistake you must not make. Even though the major metrics are certainly important, it doesn't mean you can ignore the other smaller metrics. The smaller metrics tend to provide actionable insight into how you can easily improve your sales funnel. For instance, say you notice that the overall conversion rate of traffic on your website is 1%. This is a major metric, and it suggests that one out of every one hundred visitors to your website will convert into a customer. Though this metric provides a broad overview of how conversion is taking place, it doesn't give any insights about the areas of marketing that you must improve upon.

Now, let us assume that you go back to your sales funnel and go over it with a fine-tooth comb. When you do this, you notice that five out of every 100 visitors to the website tend to subscribe to your site using e-mails. However, only about 10% of these email subscribers tend to open the emails they receive from you. This percentage is rather low, and you must work on improving it. You can fix this by making sure that you are focusing on the major and minor metrics.

Another mistake is that a lot of business owners don't test multiple payment gateway options. An important yet tricky aspect of building a sales funnel is selecting the right payment gateway for your business. The ideal method of payment for a business in the real estate industry will be quite different from that ideal for a business in the e-commerce industry. Another hurdle you will need to deal with is choosing the right number of gateways you can use. If you select too few, then it can lead to congestion in the sales funnel, and you will not be able to accommodate all your prospects easily. If you have too many, then you might scare away any potential leads due to the excess choice you provide them with. The solution to this problem is to keep testing the different permissible payment gateway options regularly. You can try coming up with different combinations of payment gateways and select a combination that works well for your business. The most popular payment gateways available these days are PayPal, Google wallet, Stripe, WePay, and Braintree.

Conclusion

I want to thank you once again for choosing this book. I hope it proved to be a helpful and enjoyable read.

Developing a sales funnel is quintessential to ensure the success of your marketing campaigns. The sales funnel has certainly become a marketing buzzword these days, but seldom do people know what it essentially entails. A fully automated and well-curated sales funnel can help increase the rate of conversions while improving your customer relations. These are two key factors that directly influence your business's bottom line.

There are certain problems that prevent a business from performing optimally. As a business owner, you might be faced with the lack of time, the absence of a properly focused and targeted social media campaign, or even the lack of understanding of the simple fact that your sales depend on you. The good news is, you no longer have to worry about these problems holding you back from doing your best.

By implementing the simple steps and by following the suggestions given in this book, you will be able to successfully create, implement, and manage an automated sales funnel that will help increase your leads along with conversion rate. Follow the different steps given to thoroughly research and create a fully functional sales funnel that will push your potential customers toward fulfilling your goal: making a purchase. The examples, along with actionable steps given in this book, will help you along the way. Also, all the suggestions given in this book are cost-effective and quite practical.

So, all that's left for you to do is get started as soon as you possibly can and make the most of a good sales funnel!

Some further reading to consider for an expanded view of some of the topics discussed include two books also written by myself, see below links to amazon.

- <u>Facebook Marketing and Advertising for Small Business Owners in 2019</u>
- <u>Instagram Marketing and Advertising for Small Business Owners in 2019</u>

You will get practical, time and money-saving advice to set up your Sales Funnel on the specific Social Media Platforms.

Dear Reader,

As an independent author,
   and one-man operation
   - my marketing budget is next to zero.

As such, the only way
   I can get my books in front of valued customers
   is with reviews.

Unfortunately, I'm competing against authors and
   giant publishing companies
   with multi-million-dollar marketing teams.

These behemoths can afford
   to give away hundreds of free books
   to boost their ranking and success.

Which as much as I'd love to –
   I simply can't afford to do.

That's why your honest review
   will not only be invaluable to me,
     but also to other readers on Amazon.

Yours sincerely,

Mark Warner

References

Horne, K. (2019). 9 Awesome Social Media Tools That Your Business REALLY Needs in 2019. Retrieved from https://digital.com/blog/social-media-tools/

The Importance of Knowing Your Customer | GROW. (2019). Retrieved from https://www.growbusiness.org/the-importance-of-knowing-your-customer/

Kolowich, L. (2019). 20 Questions to Ask When Creating Buyer Personas [Free Template]. Retrieved from https://blog.hubspot.com/marketing/buyer-persona-questions

Kirby, M. (2019). 5 Major Benefits of Creating Personas for Marketing. Retrieved from https://blog.roket.to/5-major-benefits-of-creating-personas-for-marketing

Marta, M. (2019). How to Measure Your Social Media Campaign. Retrieved from https://brand24.com/blog/measure-social-media-campaign/

Patel, N. (2019). The 5 Easy Steps To Measure Your Social Media Campaigns. Retrieved from https://neilpatel.com/blog/social-media-measurement/

Sukhraj, R. (2019). 10 Social Media KPIs You Should Track and Monitor. Retrieved from https://www.impactbnd.com/blog/social-media-kpis

Sutevski, D., & Foster, S. (2019). 4 Most Important Sales

Funnel Metrics You Need to Follow. Retrieved from https://www.entrepreneurshipinabox.com/261/the-most-important-metrics-of-the-sales-funnel/

Tien, S. (2018). How to Create a Social Media Content Calendar: Tips and Templates. Retrieved from https://blog.hootsuite.com/how-to-create-a-social-media-content-calendar/

Made in the USA
Middletown, DE
09 March 2021

35110529R00090